SAP QM Interview Questions, Answers, and Explanations: SAP Quality Management Certification Review

SAPCOOKBOOK

SAP QM Interview Questions, Answers, and Explanations

Please visit our website at www.sapcookbook.com

© 2006 Equity Press all rights reserved.

ISBN 1-933804-16-5

All rights reserved. No part of this publication may be reproduced, stored in a retrieval system, or transmitted in any form or by any means, electronic, mechanical, photocopying, recording or otherwise, without either the prior written permission of the publisher or a license permitting restricted copying in the United States or abroad.

The programs in this book have been included for instructional value only. They have been tested with care but are not guaranteed for any particular purpose. The publisher does not offer any warranties or representations not does it accept any liabilities with respect to the programs.

Trademark notices

SAP, SAP ABAP, Netweaver, and SAP New Dimension are registered trademarks of SAP AG. This publisher gratefully acknowledges SAP permission to use its trademark in this publication. SAP AG is not the publisher of this book and is not responsible for it under any aspect of the law.

SAP QM Interview Questions, Answers, and Explanations

Introduction to Quality Management 9
Question 1: Reversing the Usage Decision document 13
Question 2: Inspection Origin 05 Movement types 14
Question 3: Automatic usage decision and stock movements 15
Question 4: Inspection Lot Status 16
Question 5: Inspection lot creation 17
Question 6: Quality planning after GR 18
Question 7: Result Transfer 19
Question 8: Invoice quantity 20
Question 9: Two inspection lots created for source inspection 21
Question 10: Stock postings not yet completed for lot 23
Question 11: User as default partner in Notification 26
Question 12: MIC Long text history 27
Question 13: Regarding + ve check in In-process Inspection 28
Question 14: Process order problem W.R.T Inspection lot 30
Question 15: Collective Usage Decision 31
Question 16: Quality Certificate against delivery-QC20 33
Question 17: Extra posting proposal in UD 35
Question 18: Payment control question 36
Question 19: QM Certificates 38
Question 20: Shelf life monitoring 39
Question 21: Inspection of material for different vendors 41

3

SAP QM Interview Questions, Answers, and Explanations

Question 22: Missing attachments in notification (QM01)... 42
Question 23: Different inspection interval when retesting a material 43
Question 24: Change Inspection Stock of material in QM Only 45
Question 25: Cancel a production confirmation with inspection point.. 46
Question 26: Table for upper limit 47
Question 27: User Exit for Vendor Evaluation....... 48
Question 28: Customer - material combination inspection plan in 04 inspection type 49
Question 29: BDC_OPEN_GROUP, lock date./. is invalid 50
Question 30: Validity date of inspection plans 51
Question 31: Report stating the PO number and pending Inspection Lot Number............................. 53
Question 32: Regarding sample size...................... 55
Question 33: Automatic Creation of inspection lots (89) 57
Question 34: Skip lots... 58
Question 35: Changing the status of an inspection lot after completion 59
Question 36: Error in return delivery to vendor... 60
Question 37: QM tables.. 61
Question 38: Delete COA Profile while in Release status... 62
Question 39: Batches in QM 63
Question 40: Automatic lot creation for movement type.. 64
Question 41: Vendor blocked for quality reasons. 66
Question 42: Usage decision................................... 68
Question 43: Assigning inspection type to inspection origin.. 69
Question 44: Vendor blocked for quality reasons 71

SAP QM Interview Questions, Answers, and Explanations

Question 45: Question about workflow of QM...... 72
Question 46: Batch status 74
Question 47: Operation wise UD............................ 75
Question 48: Material Spec-Usage 76
Question 49: Manual Valuation for MIC 77
Question 50: Different material type for same material.. 78
Question 51: External processing inspection 80
Question 52: Cancellation of inspection lots......... 81
Question 53: Deactivate QM inspection 82
Question 54: Two inspection lots generated for customer returns. 83
Question 55: Problem with batch generation........ 84
Question 56: Automatic closing of lots with origin 03... 86
Question 57: QM in Delivery (SD) 88
Question 58: Function " Inspector Qualification " (QS34). 89
Question 59: Close Production Order 91
Question 60: Poor Quality Production................... 93
Question 61: Mass changes in routes 95
Question 62: Long Term Inspection....................... 97
Question 63: Serial numbers in UD........................ 98
Question 64: Expired material to block stock 99
Question 65: Confirmation profiles in Quality Notifications.. 100
Question 66: Recording Defects for UD............... 102
Question 67: Automate Inspection Points........... 103
Question 68: QM in Production........................... 106
Question 69: Digital Signatures and COA's 108
Question 70: Changing Character Results after UD? 110
Question 71: CPK value on a weekly/ daily basis 111
Question 72: Inspection Sample 112

5

SAP QM Interview Questions, Answers, and Explanations

Question 73: Percentage inspection with points. 114
Question 74: No Inspection Lot after GR Production Order 115
Question 75: Certificate results 116
Question 76: Activate inspection for SD 117
Question 77: Inspection Plan Header 118
Question 78: Valuation for inspection point 119
Question 79: Contact in Quality for Q4 121
Question 80: Collective inspection lot for batch 123
Question 81: Initial Load of QI Stock 125
Question 82: Generate a new inspection lot 126
Question 83: User Exit for QA11 127
Question 84: Partial lots - Urgent 128
Question 85: Formula in Function Module 130
Question 86: Confirmation in result recording 131
Question 87: QM & ISO 132
Question 88: Test report analysis-changing 133
Question 89: QM Notification screen exit 134
Question 90: One GR inspection batch 135
Question 91: Change of revision level with creation of inspection lot 137
Question 92: Document flow in QM notification 138
Question 93: Inspection Activation at the time of Material Creation 139
Question 93: Inspection Lot stuck between QM & WM 140
Question 94: Quality score attached to material 141
Question 95: Block Stock to Unrestricted Stock 142
Question 96: Action Box component - Create Quality Notification 143
Question 97: Skipped inspection lots and quality certificate 145
Question 98: User defined screens in Notification 090 Customer sub screen 146

Question 99: Text for auto UD in batch record... 148
Transaction Codes 149
Important Tables 157
Question 100: QM-QN-NT: creation of quality notice with reference to invoice 168

SAP QM Interview Questions, Answers, and Explanations

Introduction to Quality Management

The QM component is integrated in crucial phases of the procurement process. It supports the procurement activities by means of functions such as:

- Vendor Evaluation
- Vendor block
- Vendor Release for requests for quotation and purchase orders
- Assigning technical delivery terms and quality assurance agreements
- Certificate processing
- Status administration of the supply relationships
- Incoming inspections
- Goods receipt inspections

If your company purchases materials from external vendors, you can implement the QM in Procurement (QM-PT-RP-PRC) component to support your procurement processes for quality assurance purposes.

If you want to implement the QM in Procurement component, your company must also use the **Purchasing (MM-PUR)** component. If you require functions for processing goods movements, you must also install the **Inventory Management (MM-IM)** component.

You can implement the QM in Procurement component as a stand-alone component or together with the Quality Inspection (QM-IM) component. As a stand-alone component, you can use all procurement functions except those for processing goods receipt inspections. To process such inspections, you need the Quality Inspection component.

Using the functions of the QM in Procurement component, you can:

- Manage quality-related information for materials, vendors, and manufacturers in quality info records
- Release or block vendors and manufacturers
- Monitor the QM systems of vendors and manufacturers
- Supply quality documents with requests for quotations and purchase orders
- Evaluate vendors on the basis of quality
- Certify vendors or manufacturers that have QM systems implemented, to reduce the inspection requirement
- Manage and release supply relationships
- Request that quality certificates be submitted with the delivered goods and monitor the receipt of these certificates
- Inspect vendor goods at vendor sites (source inspections)
- Inspect vendor goods upon receipt (goods receipt inspections)
- Manage the posted goods in inspection stock
- Block the payment of invoices until the goods have been inspected and accepted

- Process goods receipt inspections for manufacturer-specific materials
- Inspect goods that have been externally processed when they are returned in a goods receipt

SAP QM Interview Questions, Answers, and Explanations

SAP QM Interview Questions, Answers, and Explanations

Question 1: Reversing the Usage Decision document

I am having a problem with the UD that I have taken for the created Inspection Lot. The following are the steps for the goods Receipt:

1) GR Blocked stock (MVT Type -103);
2) Release GR Block Stock (My Type -105);
The stock is there in the Quality and the Inspection Lot is created;
3) I did all the QA11 and took the Usage decision on that inspection Lot. Once I have taken the Usage decision, the stock gets shifted to the Unrestricted Area.

How do I reverse the Usage Decision Document?

A. If you use 322, it is trying to create a new inspection lot. If you have inspection type 08 active, it will move into QI stock and create another inspection lot.

Instead, you can try canceling the original movement document that transferred the material out of QI stock.

13

Question 2: Inspection Origin 05 Movement types

Which movement types refer to inspection origin 05?

I've also noticed that 451 refer to origin 05. Is it 5xx?

Do all movement types in Transaction Code MB1C refer to origin 05?

A. You need to check the T156S-QSSHK. It shows the inspection lot origin for all movement types. There you can find the answers to your queries.

Question 3: Automatic usage decision and stock movements

I have executed massive automatic usage decision via QA16 and noticed that no stock postings been updated. The system noted the usage decision but didn't carry any goods movements.

Why were the stock postings not updated?

Is it possible to execute in mass via QA16?

A. You should make sure that the UD codes you use have the automatic postings setup for it. The selected set code needs to be set for background postings and what material status it should post to. Take care of these and it will take care of the problems.

Question 4: Inspection Lot Status

Is anyone aware of the standard SAP function module that sets the status of an inspection lot?

I need to change the status of a lot based on certain conditions and looked at QFPO_POST_STATUS_FOR_LOT but this didn't return anything.

I need the status of the lot to be INSP RREC so that I can forward the result copy on to batch classification.

A. In general, forcing a change to the system status is not a very good idea. Instead, you should consider using a user status. If the system status is not RREC then, there will be no results to copy.

Question 5: Inspection lot creation

Is it possible to make the inspection lot quantity to (1) all the time?

Can it be configured as an automatic default in QA01?

If yes, what are the steps necessary to make a sample size default every time we create an inspection lot?

A. If you are referring to the Sample Size the answer is yes.

If you are referring to the Lot Size, then the answer is no.

For the lot quantity, you can use a sampling procedure of type fixed and assign the size to 1.

SAP QM Interview Questions, Answers, and Explanations

Question 6: Quality planning after GR

In our plant, GR for a material was made three months back. This material is QM managed. The quality plan for this material was made this month only.
Hence our QM personnel are not able to clear this particular GR.

How do I go about it?

What is the TCode for it and how do I proceed?

A. You can reset the Sample Calculation and Recalculate the change in Start & Inspection end date in QA02.

In QA02 you can also change the key date on the second tab so it looks for a plan on that date. If that plan has already been created, you can then change the key date to the current date and it will find the plan.

Question 7: Result Transfer

How do I transfer the results from one origin to another origin?

A. This can be done by creating a program attached to the follow up functions for the UD code. Once the UD is done the results can be transferred from lot to lot

Question 8: Invoice quantity

I had a Problem at doing MIRO.

For example:

My GR qty was 1000;
My Lot Qty was 1000;

After quality inspection I posted 900 in unrestricted and the remaining 100 in reserve so at the time the system was showing invoice quantity as 1000.

My FI people would like MIRO, at the same time, have the system automatically take the quantity which I posted in unrestricted.

Is this possible?

If so, how can this be accomplished?

If some other quantity should reflect in invoice quantity does it mean I should put it in rejected or should I return it to vendor quantity?

A. It is not possible to restrict invoice quantity, since reservation movement does not create any accounting documents.

If you post the quantity back to vendor, (in QA11/QA12 Stock Posting) the invoice should get updated.

Question 9: Two inspection lots created for source inspection

We encountered a problem in the source inspected material.
It creates inspection lot with inspection type 0130 for source inspection material through qi07 transaction manually against a particular purchase order. The problem is, the inspection lot is created automatically with goods inspection type 01 for the same purchase order when the material is received.

When we check with Q-info record it has a lead time set for one day. We also checked the material master for quality setting and found that it has both inspection types 01 and 0130 as well.

But the creation of two inspection lots for the same material, batch, and purchase order is not happening for all materials. It will happen randomly.

Will this setting in material master cause the second inspection lot creation for goods receipt?

Does the lead time causes this effect?

What could be the cause for this and how do I solve it?

A. You can check your Q-info record. In the area where you define the inspection type to use for the source inspection, there is an indicator "source inspection - no GR". If that is on, there is no GR (01 inspection type) created.

Question 10: Stock postings not yet completed for lot

I have a problem regarding "Stock postings not yet completed for lot".

Here's my scenario:

I have a PO having one line. I GRd it and 1000PCs goes to QI. When I view the delivery tab, the stock type is set to unrestricted use for that line item.

Actually, I have already done mvt type 321 (from QI to unrestricted) for the 1000 pieces and that 1000 pieces have already been issued.

My problem is, I have an inspection lot of 1000pc in QI shown in QVM3. When I go to QVM3, an inspection lot is shown there and I tried to release the 1000 piece QI stock to unrestricted and I got an error:

"1,000 pieces incorrect posting to unrestricted use stock, error message: Deficit of BA Stock in quality inspection 1,000 piece"

This is because I have already used up the 1000 pieces.

So I tried to record UD via QVM3. After that, it disappears in QVM3. But it appears in QVM where there is another message:

SAP QM Interview Questions, Answers, and Explanations

"Stock postings not yet completed for lot" beside the inspection .end date.

Weird thing is that I have done mvt 321 successfully and moved the QI stock to unrestricted but it still remains unreleased in qvm3 or qvm2.

I need the lot to disappear in qvm2, how do I do it?

Can I cancel it without adversely affecting the rest of my stock?

Does canceling the lot solve my problem?

Doing this in QVM2 > Usage Decision > Functions > Cancel the Lot?

A. Check the Material Documents posted for that Inspection Lot. It may give some input as to how the errors came about.

The system will also not allow the 321 in MB1B with reference to the Inspection Lot. You cannot use MB* transactions to move Inspection Stocks related with a Inspection Lot.

Try canceling that material document (321) and Repost using QA12.

Or, an alternative would be instead of doing QVM3, transfer the posting via mb1b. Resolve the issue by using mb1a mvt 552 (scrapping) then move it to QI. Once you have the stocks in QI, you can now release it in qvm3. After releasing, write off the stocks via mb1a mvt 551.

Question 11: User as default partner in Notification

I want the system to take my user name as default for partner AO Author while creating a notification. I've created the partner determination profile and assigned it to the notification but it is not defaulting the user name as partner.

What can I do to correct this?

A. I assume that you have an organization for the partners. I think you need to utilize workflow and do some coding.

Utilize the user ids. Use the KU for coordinator since it is for the user, and KO is for the person which requires HR. When a Q3 based notification is created the coordinator would be defaulted. But as I said, it requires organization, workflow and some coding.

Question 12: MIC Long text history

Where does the system store MIC long text history?

When I tried using, 'Read_text function module', the system is fetching only new long text.

How do I fetch the old long text of MIC?

A. The system does not store the long text history, because it is a text. To maintain the long text, create MIC with the appropriate versions and assign MIC in the task list as per the required version. The setting is in customization for the plant level, MIC with history.

An alternative recourse is to check out AUT10. You need to set it up, but it allows you track changes to any Long Text. I believe it is available from 4.5 or 4.6.

Question 13: Regarding + ve check in In-process Inspection

For a particular product we have six (6) different stages. I have added a few MICs on Operation/Phase no. 40 in TCode C202 so that I can record results for Inprocess Inspection.
I have the following two queries:

1. While taking UD for this Inprocess Inspection, I cannot subtract sample quantity because the 'Inspection Lot Stock' tab doesn't appear. How can I subtract samples for this Inprocess Inspection lot?

2. It was decided that the Inprocess Inspection will not be a +ve check (i.e. even if I reject a particular operation, the PP person can go ahead with the next operation). I just want for a particular product, that the Inprocess Inspection should be a +ve check i.e. unless I approve this operation. The PP person should not be able to proceed to the next operation.

How do I accomplish this?

A. First of all, there will be no Stock posting tab for 03 type inspection lot. It is controlled by PP for posting inventory (i.e. goods receipt) by appropriate control key for an operation.

During the confirmation by PP, they can declare the scrap/sample quantity, which is for reporting/costing and not inventory.

The second point to be controlled by control key for an operation confirmation setting. Try it.

Question 14: Process order problem W.R.T Inspection lot

Why can't the process set deletion flag? The system gives a message that inspection lot is still open.

What do I do with the inspection lot?

Should I cancel it? If so, is it possible?

Note: Usage decision is not made yet.

What is the procedure to cancel the inspection lot?

A. It's inspection type 03. Try QA02 and change inspection lot.

In there you can cancel the inspection lot.

If it is production order CO02, go to functions --> Inspection Lot --> delete and save. The inspection lot will be deleted. Then set the deletion flag for the order.

Question 15: Collective Usage Decision

When I execute the TC:QA16 it is not showing any Inspection Lot. But there are many Inspection lots which are matching the selected criteria.

I have looked into the Material Master Auto usage decision which has been ticked (checked), even though I haven't checked it. What could be the reasons for this?

Why is the inspection lot not displayed? Are there any settings I need to make to have them displayed?

I have checked all the conditions i.e.

Characteristic processing is completed. - i.e. Status 5
No usage decision has been made.
No characteristics have been rejected.
No defects have been recorded.

Even after all the conditions are met it is not displaying any Inspection lot. What may be the other reasons for this?

A. Check if all the characteristics in the inspection lot have been valuated and are completed - status 5.

Also verify whether the lot is created with inspection point, because collective UD cannot be made for a lot with further inspection (Inspection point).

Question 16: Quality Certificate against delivery- QC20

I am facing a typical problem while I try to generate a COA against a delivery.

I have created a certificate profiled and assigned it to Material/customer.

I have produced a batch and recorded the result and done the UD.

I have created a delivery for the same batch. I have maintained the setting required for the output type LQCB.

I have also created the recipient using transaction VV22.

Still I am not able to generate the COA against delivery.

There is a message saying 'No messages'.

I am sure I am missing some settings in the output type.

What do I do to correct this and what are the steps I need to do for the output type setting?

SAP QM Interview Questions, Answers, and Explanations

A. First, you need to create a Q-infoset. Then, create one with transaction QV51.

Question 17: Extra posting proposal in UD

Can somebody explain to me how a new posting proposal can be added in order to use this in the catalog assigned to a UD code?

There is a new one but won't be available (VMENGE01) until 2007.

I want to add an extra one.

A. Try the customizing path Quality Management --> Quality Inspection --> Inspection Lot completion --> Define inventory postings.

Question 18: Payment control question

The process for payment in our company is as follows:

'GR--QI--accept or return---if accept payment'.

Before, we control the payment as 'first GR with movement type 103', and if the quality is satisfactory we use 105 to receive it. Related people can compare the invoice quantity with the GR quantity and do related payment.

Last month, we implemented a new QM module and with the QM module we only can use movement type 101 to do goods received. With this, we could not compare GR quantity with invoice quantity to do payment. We also had to check individually before the payment. This process takes time and could easily cause mistakes.

Is there a better way of doing this?

A. To handle the GR, check the configuration to see if QM is active for movement 105.

Now that you've switched on QM you should do both 103 & 105 to get the stock in QI, and keep it there for your quality inspection.

The check you're talking about can be managed by switching on QM in procurement and using QM Control key 0007 (in the Material Master).
The system will then block the invoice while the stock is in QI. If the batch is approved the block will be removed.

SAP QM Interview Questions, Answers, and Explanations

Question 19: QM Certificates

The deletion flag on Production Order was set but had to be revoked to allow further goods issues. Issues have now taken place but in trying to reset the deletion flag, the following error message occurs. "The order has been flagged with delivery complete".

What are the settings necessary for generating Quality certificates in SAP?

A. You're normally not allowed to mark a Production order for deletion as long as the financial value on the order isn't zero and/or you've got materials posted to it.

I can't see the point in deleting an order with postings. That way you'd probably mess up both logistics and accounting.

Question 20: Shelf life monitoring

I have a scenario of monitoring the shelf life for the material.
As such, I have maintained the following settings:

a) Shelf life and batch data in Plant data 1 (MM01);
b) 09 inspection type for QM view in MM01;
c) Activated movement type for the plant OMJ5;

Still I face some problem in monitoring the shelf life. The inspection lot is not being generated after the expiration of the period.

The batches are being posted to Blocked stock. No inspection lot is getting generated automatically.

Is there any way to post the material to the QI stock so the lot will be generated automatically?

Is there some other setting that has to be maintained?

A. Maintain inspection interval in material master. Check if the stock is available for that material or not. Then execute dead line monitoring of the batch in transaction qa07.

You can also check the next inspection date in the batch master. Unless it was setup for recurring inspection when you did the original 01, this date may not be populated.

You can also check your indicators in QA07 to insure you have the inspection lot and block option checked. Also check the expiration date. The expiration date should be checked before the next inspection date.

Question 21: Inspection of material for different vendors

I have a requirement from a client for inspection of a material for different vendors. Characteristics change from vendor to vendor. Automatically, the inspection plan will need to be selected based on the vendor.

How do I accomplish this?

A. In the material to plan assignment, scroll to the right and you will see a vendor column. If you put a vendor number in that column, that is the plan that will be selected for the material/plant/vendor.

Question 22: Missing attachments in notification (QM01)

I know it should be possible to attach files, pictures etc. when creating notifications. However, I am working right know in an automotive release and cannot find the button anymore.

Did we miss something?

What can be wrong?

A. Check what type of user you have set up. Sometimes the security guys set up a testing ID as a different type than a regular user. Some ID types don't have the ability to use the Object services functionality.

Question 23: Different inspection interval when retesting a material

We have a requirement to use reduced inspection duration when we re-test a batch of a material.

For example when we first test a batch that has just been manufactured, the inspection duration is two years so the batch gets a next inspection date two years into the future.

When we retest this material in the future (as it approaches the next inspection date), we want to use an inspection duration of only 50% of the original inspection duration (one year in this example). So the batch gets a new next inspection date one year into the future. This applies to all re-tests (to only use 50% of the defined inspection duration).

As there is only one field in the material master for the inspection interval (in the QM view) I do not know of any way of achieving this in SAP.

How do I resolve this problem?

A. For re-test you have to use inspection plans with usage code 9. So for these plans, you can create your specific requirements separate from the plans related to usage 1 (production).

Alternatively, there is actually a user-exit (QEVA0003) available where the system calculates the next inspection date. You just need to write the program to calculate the next date.

Question 24: Change Inspection Stock of material in QM Only

I have activated 04 Inspection type with post to Inspection stock for a material.

I have left QM not active unchecked for 101 Mvt type for Mvt Indicator F (GR for Order) in OMJJ.

While I am doing GR for the Process Order, the '101' message appears.

What is the problem and how can I resolve this?

A. If the process order was created after you modified the material, then it's an "old" process order, and this may explain the error.

If there was an existing stock of this material before you start, then try this first with a newly created material. Afterwards, the error you describe should not happen.

SAP QM Interview Questions, Answers, and Explanations

Question 25: Cancel a production confirmation with inspection point.

I'm using transaction QE11 to confirm production orders (inspection point by shift '120') and to save defects. The problem is that I can not reverse these production confirmations with transaction CO13 as I do normally in PP.

How I can cancel this production confirmation to delete 101 for the production and 261 for all the raw materials?

Note: I don't want a reverse material document.

A. For technical and logical reasons, you cannot reverse an integrated production confirmation with inspection points and auto GR. Instead, you have to reverse the material document.

An alternative solution is to enter again in transaction QE11 the inspection point. Put to reverse indicate "non confirmation". In this way the PP confirmation is reversed.

Question 26: Table for upper limit

In the inspection plan I have a characteristic with upper limit.

In which table can I find this value?

A. Look at table PLMK.

If it is a reference MIC, also check QPMK.

These are for checking the plan. The Inspection Lot keeps them in different values.

Question 27: User Exit for Vendor Evaluation

I am using exit MM06L001 (Function Module-EXIT_SAPMM06L_001) for quality criteria. The scores of the sub criteria are calculated on the basis of quality notifications and inspection lots. But no score is getting calculated for the vendor.

Where did I go wrong and what can I do to remedy the error?

A. Regarding quality notification, do verify the following:

a. Notification completed with External origin.
b. Invoice verification already took place.

As for inspection lot, verify that usage decision has been made. In addition, verify customization of all required parameters (as listed in documentation under QM->Quality Control->Vendor Evaluation).

Question 28: Customer - material combination inspection plan in 04 inspection type

I have one issue. I have in my plant discrete manufacturing which makes two orders. It is production based on sales order. Inspection is based on the customer mentioned in the sales order.

How do I create different inspection plans according to customer - material combination with inspection type 04?

Another requirement is at different stages of production down the BOM level. The inspection should be done for the same customer and the plan should be attached to the GR (04) automatically at all the stages, according to that customer.

How can I fulfill this requirement?

A. You can create different task lists in the same group and same usage with different group counters. Now while in the task overview screen, choose menu inspection plan->material T-List assignment. As a table pops up, you can specify which task list applies to which customer. You can also create multiple entries for the same group counter and with different customers.

SAP QM Interview Questions, Answers, and Explanations

Question 29:
BDC_OPEN_GROUP, lock date./. is invalid

When I try to upload data with LSMW to create inspection plan, the system shows the message:

"BDC_OPEN_GROUP, lock date./. is invalid".

I have BDC authority, so what's the problem?

A. Did you enter a date for field START in structure BI000? The date has to be earlier than today's date.

The queue start date specifies the day until which a batch input folder is locked. You cannot process a locked batch input folder until the day after the specified date.

Question 30: Validity date of inspection plans

We have a problem where inspection plans have to be maintained as counter one with e.g. four characteristics. A second plan, counters two, has a fifth characteristic and should be valid from e.g. next week and for the next two weeks. After that period, plan counter one has to be valid again.

How this can be maintained?

Is there a chance to maintain the "valid to-date" in the plan header?

I tried to change an inspection plan with change number, but I only had the possibility to maintain the Valid from date. The valid date is still 31.12.9999.

What could be wrong and how could this be corrected?

A. Check the engineering change functionality in SAP.

On Header level you can select the change mode (only with change number). With those change numbers you can plan and maintain changes of the inspection plan in advance.

SAP QM Interview Questions, Answers, and Explanations

You can also try using one inspection plan and use this functionality. In this case you will have only one plan (Header and Counter) but via the Valid until date more "plans". You will see how the plan looks like for a certain period.

For your last question, create an ECN with effectively type DATE. (Effectively, type is to be specified in the opening screen itself). Then enter effectively intervals (shift+F9), and there you are.

Question 31: Report stating the PO number and pending Inspection Lot Number

I am doing quality after doing Migo MVt Type 105. So when the Migo Mvt Type105 doc is saved then the inspection lot is generated and the stock is in Quality.

Can you tell me the transaction code for the stock on which the usage decision is pending? It should tell me the PO number also.

A. You can use the list display transaction code QE51N and in the EXCEPTION criteria you can specify it to be 'UD Not done'.

Otherwise in the same transaction code QE51N in the output columns, you can display the column "Usage decision by" and sort by it so that the blank ones are on the top. Those blank ones are the lots for which UD was not done. Once you find out the lot numbers you can open the lot and see the order number in it.

QVM3 is the most suitable t-code to find such lots.

Alternately, t-code QA11 has an opening screen with a button: Lots without UD. Give your selection criteria there and execute. In the list that is generated, click on the inspection lot number and you are taken to the inspection lot details screen, which shows, among other things, the PO, the production order or the sales order number. Whichever applies for you.

Question 32: Regarding sample size

I have a packing material whose unit of measurement (UOM) is THS.

Our sampling system is that when the incoming quantity of material is between 1 NOS to 100 NOS we take 1 NOS samples. Between 101 NOS to 2000 NOS we take 20 NOS samples and above it we take a fix of 30 NOS samples. Now these limits are in NOS and the sample quantity which I mentioned is also in NOS. I have given the alternate UOM as NOS in the material master with the equation 1000 NOS = 1 THS.

While creating the sampling scheme if I want to mention the lot size in NOS, I will have to use decimals i.e. I have to write 0.001 THS instead of 1 NOS and the sampling scheme doesn't allow me to enter lot size or sample size in decimals.

How do I create a sampling scheme which can fulfill this criterion of mine and how do I attach it to the quality plan?

A. Do not disturb the sampling scheme. Let it be like this:

Upto 100 units: 1
Upto 200 units: 20

Upto (say) 100000 units: 30

Now, in the 'sample' tab for inspection characteristics, mention the sample unit of measure as NOS and base sample quantity as 1.

Question 33: Automatic Creation of inspection lots (89)

Is there a way to create inspection lot programmatically in an ABAP Report?

Is there any Business object, function module or user exit?

We went to 1 lot for 1 shift. We use inspection origin 89 (manual). Therefore we're searching for a way to create the inspection lot via job (ABAP program).

How do I resolve this?

A. Automatic creation of Inspection lot in SAP is governed by Inspection lot origin, inspection type, etc.

You have to give the details of why you want an inspection lot creation by program or ABAP report.

Instead, you can use a report/program to do it. Standard SAP provides this functionality.

If it is in--process inspection, you can use inspection points based on shifts.

Question 34: Skip lots

I was in the process of testing the scenario of skip lots. I have done all the data maintenance in the material master and the dynamic modification rule. The quality level is getting updated to a skip stage, but the stock is not getting directly put into unrestricted stock when the lot should be skipping.

Where am I going wrong and how do I correct this?

A. This can be done by setting the Control Inspection lot indicator in the QM view of the material master to each material document.

Iit works for DMR at a lot and characteristic level.

Question 35: Changing the status of an inspection lot after completion

We have two inspection lots for which UD has already been done. Later on we realized that these lots the sample size was not calculated. Now we want to reset the "Sample Calculation" but not able as the status of the lot is "UD done".

Is there a way we can reverse UD or reset the status of an inspection lot?

A. Under normal condition, a UD cannot be reversed.

Question 36: Error in return delivery to vendor

I could not create return delivery for a material. The message display is:

'COULD NOT CREATE RETURN DELIVERY WM MOVEMENT TYPE 102 NOT ALLOWED FOR WAREHOUSE NO. 010'.

How do I fix this problem?

A. Check in the configuration. The message clearly says that for the Warehouse no. 010 you have not allowed movement type "102".

You have to change this configuration and add a line or move the stock to a warehouse where customer returns are allowed.

Question 37: QM tables

How do I populate additional entries directly into the tables?

Is there any direct way to populate fields in the tables?

A. It depends on which tables you are talking about because some tables can be directly maintained in PRD. For some you have to transport it maintaining in DEV system. For example, number ranges are not transportable. You have to maintain it directly in every instance.

If you are talking about mass maintenance, Standard SAP QM does not have it by now. You can talk to your developer to write a program for you by which you can do a mass maintenance. Otherwise SM30 is good enough to run.

Question 38: Delete COA Profile while in Release status

I have created some Certificate Profiles that need to be deleted. But they are all in released status. I know that Certificate Profile cannot be deleted if it is in "REL" status.

How I should deal with this issue?

A. It seems to me you could potentially block the profile - from within the profile, edit -> block profile.

Once it's blocked, you can proceed with the deletion.

Question 39: Batches in QM

I need some guidelines in maintaining the settings for batch management in QM.

What are the customizations necessary for batch management from QM point of view?

How the inspection lots get triggered and how are they connected / interlinked to the batches?

A. The links have to do with your configuration of batch management for your material. If the materials in question are batch managed and are purchased or manufactured within your organization when the material is received using the 101 movement type, the batch is created and assigned in the background to the inspection lot.

Depending on how you've designed your inspection plan or material specification, you can build the master inspection characteristics, dependent on class characteristics, that will copy the inspection results into the batch record.

This is less QM configuration than it is MM-Batch Management configuration and material master definition.

SAP QM Interview Questions, Answers, and Explanations

Question 40: Automatic lot creation for movement type

There's a specific scenario for my client.

During production, only for the rejection from production department (during confirmation), QC wants to play a role.

So we propose this:

When there's a rejection, production department will move the stock manually to QI and in case of acceptance it will move to unrestricted.

Can inspection lots be generated automatically at the time of movement to QI?

A. If the requirement in your case is that:

1. The inspection lot will be created after inspection i.e. the lot will be created with the quantity inspected and rejected quantity when production is taking place then the only solution is to create the inspection lot "Automatically".

2. The reason being by standard SAP there is no control provided at the level of "Movement types" for "Automatic creation of inspection lots".

3. Standard SAP assumes that there can't be an inspection without an inspection lot.

In your case you are physically doing the inspection without creating an inspection lot and you want to create a lot only if there's a rejection. Standard SAP does not consider it to be a good practice and hence does not support automatic creation of Inspection lot at this stage.

4. However SAP does not stop you from creating a manual lot at any stage and perform an inspection.

Question 41: Vendor blocked for quality reasons

I am getting an error message while creating a scheduling agreement with one vendor:

"Vendor blocked for quality reasons"

Message no. 06884

Diagnosis:

Quality Management has blocked this vendor as a source of supply for this material."

How do I activate this vendor again?

A. Go to the relevant quality info record (QI02) and see if the vendor can be released from there.

Go to the "Vendor master change TCODE 'XK02". Once the vendor master is displayed, go to the menu function "Extras-->Blocked data". On this screen there is a section at the end for "Block for quality reasons". The field "Block function" must have been filled with some code like "99/**". Just blank out this field and save the data and the vendor will be released.

However as a good practice you might want to check with "Quality/Purchasing" department if they have knowingly blocked the vendor, as receiving against a blocked vendor is not allowed in many companies.

SAP QM Interview Questions, Answers, and Explanations

Question 42: Usage decision

I want to post the stock from Quality Inspection to unrestricted use partially with two UD codes for same inspection lot. But the QGA2 system will show the total document posted on only one usage decision code. I want to evaluate the stock on the basis of usage decision code.

How can I resolve this issue?

A. You could use inspection points and partial lots. In this way, you may have a different UD for inspection points and inventory posting accordingly.

Question 43: Assigning inspection type to inspection origin

While customizing, I've come across setting of inspection type to inspection origin. I wondered why it is not possible to assign a specific inspection type to more than one inspection origin. I wanted to assign inspection type 06 to inspection origin 05 and 06 but a error message appeared.

The funny thing is, that one inspection origin can have several inspection types. What is it used for?

A. The inspection lot origin is a key used by SAP to determine from where an inspection came from or what the source is.

In the case of inspection lot origin 01, any inspection related to this origin came from a purchase order or contract (e.g., a scheduling agreement). A lot is generated under this origin, delivered, and are numbered beginning with 01.

However, because multiple types of inspection may be possible for inspections originating from purchases, the origin includes several inspection types. Delivered, you'll find regular, series inspection and the first article or pilot inspection types. The system controls these through status management in the quality info record. Regardless of the type of inspection, however, all 01 origin inspection lots are numbered beginning 01 and require vendor/PO data as part of the inspection lot creation.

Moving an existing inspection type from one origin to another won't work, because the inspection types also have their own default values in the IMG that are relevant to the origins. You're better off creating additional inspection types manually, but for the most part, SAP has created the standards one would need to implement the inspection process.

Question 44: Vendor blocked for quality reasons

I am getting an error message while creating scheduling agreement with one vendor:

Vendor blocked for quality reasons

Message no. 06884

Diagnosis

Quality Management has blocked this vendor as a source of supply for this material.

How do I activate this vendor again?

A. QInfo Record (Transaction: QI02) should be the best starting point.

Or else check in the Vendor Master.

Question 45: Question about workflow of QM

I've a problem about quality notification.

When I release a task in the quality notification, the person that I specify in the response can't receive the workflow task item in his workplace. I've activated the event link in the customizing of QN.

Why doesn't it work?

If I use this function, what steps should I do?

A. You'll need to maintain the Workflow. Even though SAP supply lots of 'finished' WF's ready to use, there's always something to adjust or set up.

The Agent Assignment has to be maintained for the task in the WF.

If you've got a WF responsible in your company you should talk to her/him. If not, you might have to try doing it yourself.

Maintaining a WF in the 'Workflow builder' isn't impossible. Try transaction SWDD. Enter the WF number (Use Structure search to find the relevant WF) and press the 'Check button'. You'll get some messages in the field at the bottom of the screen. All error messages and also the information messages about Agents you'll have to take care of to get the WF working. If you click on the message the system will take you to where you need to maintain.

When you're through handling all messages you'll have to activate the WF before trying the notification again.

SAP QM Interview Questions, Answers, and Explanations

Question 46: Batch status

I would like to know where the batch status can be set in SAP. We have the stock type Q for Quality inspection. We would like stock type R for rework and S for blocked.

Where can this be set in SAP?

A. There is no way to create a new status. The only thing you can do, if you have Batch Management, is to activate the Batch status so you can have Unrestricted (blank), Quality (Q) and Blocked (S). Having these batch statuses, you can duplicate all stocks to restricted Q, blank and S.

Question 47: Operation wise UD

I am having 3 different operations. The 0020 and 0030 Operation is dependent on the 0010 operation. It means that once the RR is done for operation 0010, manual UD has to be taken immediately. Then results are recorded for operation 0020 & 0030 and finally a common UD is made for both 0020 & 0030 operation. This is the case for incoming inspection and in process inspection.

Is there any customization for this type of RR & UD?

A. You could use Inspection Points for 0010 (it has its own UD) and then use the Inspection Lot UD for the whole process.

Question 48: Material Spec-Usage

How do I use material specification?

If I want to use material specification, what are the things I should do?

A. To use Material specification you need to have:

1) Class Characteristics;
2) MIC's linked to the Class Characteristics;
3) A Class containing the Class Characteristics, assigned to the Material Master;
4) Material spec maintained. (QS61);
5) Limit values for the characteristics, maintained in the classification view in the material master;
6) Inspection with material specification chosen in the inspection type in the material master.

Question 49: Manual Valuation for MIC

While RR for some of the MIC's, the system is asking for Manual Valuation and for some it is not asking.

I want the system to ask Manual Valuation for all the MIC's.

What settings should I do to get this?

A. Check your Valuation Mode / Sampling Procedure. From there, you can find the settings needed to configure your requirement.

SAP QM Interview Questions, Answers, and Explanations

Question 50: Different material type for same material

Is it advisable to create different material type for same material?

Purpose:
One material type would be with quality active.
The other would be without quality inspection.

In case of emergency, the without quality material shall be issued to production.

What may be the disadvantages?

How can this situation be handled without creating a different material type?

A. Instead of defining a separate material for "emergency purpose", I would suggest you should skip the inspection by forcing completion on the characteristics and make a usage decision as "accepted without inspection", or something similar.

This way, there will be a record that the inspection lot was closed without inspection. The exact circumstances which qualified as emergency can be recorded in the long text for UD.

Alternatively, if it is a batch managed material, you could try using the "restricted use" status.

Failing that, if you have the samples, you can still use QA11 to post the material without making the actual usage decision. When you finish the inspection, finish the lot normally. If it fails, you will need to track down where the material was used and bring it back.

Question 51: External processing inspection

I would like to set up External processing inspection. My process is
1. Generate Production order
2. In routing.
The first operation is internal process.
The second operation is external processing, system generate PR for external processing
The third operation is internal process.

I would like to know the following:

1. What is the standard setting for this scenario?
2. Which Inspection type will we use? Should it be in-process or GR?
3. Do we use Routing or inspection plan?

A. In case you want the material should be inspected after it returns from external processing, then you must use inspection type 01, for GR against the PO that you will create for external processing. The plan for this will be different (as opposed to the routing).

Question 52: Cancellation of inspection lots

Is it possible to cancel the inspection lot once it has been created?

A. You can cancel it by reversing the transaction that created it.

It's also possible to go into the inspection lot in Chance mode and set the status to "locked". It will then disappear, but if there's QI stock linked to it you won't get it out.

SAP QM Interview Questions, Answers, and Explanations

Question 53: Deactivate QM inspection

If a material quality history is good and we would like to deactivate the inspection. Currently we know if we want to do this, no inspection lot would exist.
At the same time when we check in the purchase order position delivery view there are stock indicator X.

If we deactivate the inspection for following GR, which stock type will it be and how can it be modified?

A. If you deactivate QM in the QM view of the material you'll see that there's a field called 'Post to insp. stock' appearing.

If that is ticked. material will go to QI, but as long as QM isn't activated you can do an ordinary MM transaction MB1B or MIGO_TR with movement 321 to get it to unrestricted use.

If you remove the selection 'Post to insp. stock', stock will go to unrestricted use.

82

Question 54: Two inspection lots generated for customer returns.

I have assigned 05 as inspection type in material master and assigned 5 as usage in task list for a material. Once this material is returned from the customer (thorough SD module - returns delivery), I am getting two inspection lots generated, one with REL CALC and other with REL CALC SPRQ status.

Since I want to have the segregation of stock after UD, I want the lot with REL CALC SPRQ status only.

How can I avoid the lot which is generated with REL CALC status?

A. Since you've got one with and one without SPRQ it seems like you've got two different insp. types triggering the two lots.

Check which inst. type is triggering the inspection lot without the SPRQ, and consider deactivating it in the Material master.

Question 55: Problem with batch generation

I am using SAP 4.OB.

We are using partial lots in QM (only partial lots and no batches) but while making the Usage Decision, the system asked a for batch number (may be because of material being managed in batches). Hence, we require a batch number. I made settings in customizing for batch management and initiated batch creation at production order release, so that we can put this batch number at the usage decision.

We are using a system where batch is generated while we make GR against production order. (It will pick batch number created at order release automatically).

But we make GR for partial production order quantities so we require a different batch number for each partial quantity. However, it picks the same batch number created at order release time. Once a partial quantity with a batch number is posted, an error message will pop up indicating that batch was already posted to inventory, so that same batch number can not be used for multiple postings.

I want a separate batch number just for use in a usage decision which should not be in conflict with the batch in GR.

In GR, the batch should be created automatically for each partial production order quantity.

How can I accomplish this requirement?

A. You have contradicting logic, when you create batch at order release and the fact that you do not always want to use this batch in the case of a partial receipt. Unless the shop floor wants to print labels or papers etc., you should not create a batch with the order.

IF you are using partial lots, create a new batch for every partial lot. That would be cleaner and would fulfill your requirement.

# Question 56: Automatic closing of lots with origin 03

I can remember my consultant telling me he has set up a job running overnight that closes all lots of origin 03 if the order was confirmed.

It does not seem to work. I'd like to check this job and if necessary set it up again.

Could you give me some hint where and how I can do that?

A. Check transaction QA40. This will do what you need. Create a variant and run this on a nightly basis.

Follow the steps below:

1. Go to QA40 & check whether there are variants created. IF not, create variants as in the development server.
2. After creation of variant go to QA41 & click on each variant & click "Schedule job".
3. Enter suitable time i.e. in the night & click "schedule periodically"
4. Click on "days" radio button & press create.

This will schedule the job everyday

Repeat this process for all variants.

You can monitor each job in the transaction QA40L in which you can see a log of the periodic job & also inspection lots for which UD is done.

Question 57: QM in Delivery (SD)

We have a requirement where usage decision for an inspection lot must be completed before Packing. i.e., if user goes for a packing function in delivery, the system should validate for Inspection lot UD. If UD is not taken, the system should not allow the packing.

I know that Standard SAP offers UD check at the time of Post Goods Issue.

Is there any User exit or any validation check in QM?

A. Depending on your version, check relevant exits for transaction VL02 in
SMOD. In 4.0b you have a program MV50AFZ1 being called in the main program SAPMV50A and there is a mention to form:

"User_exit_read_document": The documentation states that this user exit can be used to read data in additional tables when the program reads a delivery.

Question 58: Function " Inspector Qualification " (QS34).

What is the use of the function "Inspector Qualification (QS34)"?

The system informs that:

1. The qualification that an inspector must have and, if necessary, validate in order to be able to conduct an inspection.
2. This field does not control other data. However, your entry is checked against a list of qualifications stored in the data base.

What does the sentence "Checked against a list of qualification stored in the data base" mean?

Is there a QM check against the HR?

A. You will have to create your own Authorization object and assign it to a relevant user authorization group.

If you go to (in 4.0b):

1) ABAP Workbench > Development > Other Tools > Authorization
Objects > Fields > Customer > Maintain table "ZAUTHCUST" (SE11):

Maintain entry for field TQ11-PRFQL.

2) ABAP Workbench > Development > Other Tools > Authorization
Objects > Objects > QA > (select relevant object OR create new one):

Attach the authorization field created previously.

3) Maintain the relevant activity group (PFCG).

Question 59: Close Production Order

My inspection lot has status 'UD' and 'LTIN'. When I close my production order for this inspection lot, it won't do it. Instead, the system suggested this:

"If an order contains inspection lots, you can only activate a deletion flag to complete the order, if each inspection lot has the status 'Completion of all inspections set' or usage decision made".

I think my inspection lot has status 'UD'. It should close the order but may be the status 'LTIN' requires longer inspection.

How can I do it?

A. This problem is caused by the usage of long term inspection characteristics in your inspection plans which allows result recording even after UD. As the UD isn't finalized for the system by using LT MIC's, related objects (in this case the production order) can't be closed or archived. The only way to get rid of this is to think about the correct usage of LT characteristics. If the usage is correct, you shouldn't close the production order.

Many users like the LT MIC, as it allows them to massage the results even after UD. But the LT MIC is clearly for those MIC's which requires longer inspection times, i.e. in case a sample needs to be analyzed by an external institute for PCB or Dixione analysis, which takes normally longer. Or you have inspections which are not relevant for quality but will be inspected later or the result is simply not available at the time of UD.

As a solution you can force the inspection completion (status LTIN will set inactive and ICCO gets active) via the automatic usage decision report (transaction QA10) where a flag for LT MIC's provides you a way to finally close the inspection lot even if there are open LT MIC's.

Question 60: Poor Quality Production

We have inspection type 04 to complete our FQA (final quality assurance). In inspection type setting we use every material document inspection. The system will give us an inspection lot when our production staff confirms the production order using co15. In a normal situation, there is no problem. The problem will occur when there is poor quality production.

Our QA staff checked some materials which had poor quality, so they want to let the production staff rework the materials. But I don't know how the system will deal with the situation.

How can I return the bad materials into the previous production order?

How can I do the second check when the bad material has been reworked?

How will production deal with it?

A. The standard process for EPC follows the way that you reject the batch with UD. That is, to perform the posting to blocked stock and classify the batch as rework stuff. Then production picks the batch and starts a new process order (rework order). This is the cleanest way because your product costing will be correct as any rework will incur additional costs. The best scenario is somehow dependent on what type of rework will be necessary. In this case it's always just minor adjustments, and then you might keep it easy and inform your production team via defect recording that something is out of specification. Use notification in those cases as well as a user exit in result recording which provides us a button to print the operation with the rejected MIC's on a relevant printer in production. You can use the planer group from the inspection plan to identify the production area.

With regards your main question, once PP confirmed the quantity, you have to deal with that in QM (assuming it will be posted to QI-stock) via the usage decision. You can not return it to the PP order. Use a new process order with its own recipe setup in a way to suit the rework process.

SAP QM Interview Questions, Answers, and Explanations

Question 61: Mass changes in routes

In our company we were using multiple characteristics for each operation, and to record 'DEFECTS' for each characteristic.

We recently switched to a new system. We previously record 'DEFECTIVES', and a used single characteristic per operation. Now, for materials created earlier to this scenario, we have to make mass changes in all the routes. We tried to run a BDC, but it is not working.

Are there other options of eliminating multiple characteristics from operations and putting a new but single characteristic for each operation?

A. Whenever you need to upload/change multi-level data like recipes, routings, and inspection plans, you better use LSMW. BDC will not work.

LSMW is a mighty tool but with mighty tools comes many settings, flags etc. It's not a 1.2.3 deal and you're done. There's a lot of transaction to start with and review over and over. It takes some time to understand how to proceed and harder still, to troubleshoot when things go wrong.

There is now a short cut for this. You just have to go through the documentation again to find the transaction error and catch it from there.

Question 62: Long Term Inspection

The long term inspection characteristic is not closed. Meanwhile, the UD system does not post quantity transfer in back ground.

What is the solution for this?

A. Even with LT characteristics you are able to perform the stock posting according to the UD-code as defined in the QM customizing. We recently had the problem where SAP enhanced the function with a 'feature' where the quantity required the open LT characteristic. It is subtracted from the posting quantity. Many users complained and SAP provided an OSS-note to set that back so that the full quantity gets posted.

Question 63: Serial numbers in UD

We are using serial numbers for finished goods we purchase. In the goods receipt we enter the serial numbers and the stock goes to QI. The inspection lot captures the S/N but when I perform a UD I will get a pop up window asking for S/N if I attempt to scrap (553 MT). It does not do it though when I block for a new material.

What am I missing here and how do I resolve it?

A. If you are trying to process the whole inspection lot quantity and if you are scrapping less than the whole Lot Quantity then the system will want to know which S/N is being scrapped. If the movement to blocked stock or other material is for the whole lot quantity then the system does need to ask for S/N.

Question 64: Expired material to block stock

I want to run a variant to post expired stock to blocked stock. But since batch status is active, current stock is changing from unrestricted to restricted and we are not able to see restricted stock from MMBE.

How do I change this setting and what are the prerequisites for posting expired material from unrestricted to block stock?

A. The deadline monitoring program is a little confusing. SAP does not move the material to blocked stock. It restricts it. There is no way to change this with out modifying the program. Copy the SAP deadline monitoring program and insert a section to do your stock moves the way you want it.

Also note that in MMBE you can control which "stock types" and "stock status" are displayed by creating/changing your "Display version" (entries in T136 and T136* either via IMG or SM32, depending on your release).

Question 65: Confirmation profiles in Quality Notifications

I am trying to apply the defect confirmation categories to the defect recording screens of manually created notifications. My customer is very strong on defect recording and I have a number of manually created notification types for various processes. I want to get away from the "standard" defect recording view as we do not need all the fields that are displayed (assembly, valuation, etc). I want to use the 0030 Confirmation profile to get just the defect type, cause and location.

How do I configure this into the notification types?

A. Check the Report Type 00000030. In this report type, you will see confirmation profile 0030. Assign a suitable catalog profile and define the origin of catalog profile i.e. Quality Notification type or Material number.

Assign this report type to your plant and work center combination. You can assign the same to all plants and all work centers. In standard SAP, you will find report type 00000042.

Assign the catalog profile which is mentioned in report type to your notification type.

You can also find inspection plans per material/plant combination transactions QP01, Qp02 and QP03.

There is also transaction CWBQM - the QM work bench. This transaction allows you to find all plans across plants. You might need to customize the work area.

The QM workbench provides full access to inspection plans in case you need to perform mass changes.

You can quickly develop a simple query in SQ01 to read table MAPL or even simply use the Quick View functionality/transaction to a straight read in this table. Other than that, the advice given before was to go through an ABAP report.

Question 66: Recording Defects for UD

When recording defects for a UD, I am selecting the relevant defects to be entered on the overview screen. When I hit enter a detail screen appears for each defect entered. I just want to have the overview screen.

How can I switch the detail screen?

A. Check the QM customizing.

IMG:
QM -> Quality Notification
-> Defects recording
-> Define Confirmation profile

There you can define what needs to be entered when dealing with defects.

In the report category, link the confirmation profile to the catalog profile. You find, that just next to it, the confirmation profile definition is in the customizing.

Question 67: Automate Inspection Points

I am working with inspection points during production (Inspection Type 03) in 4.6C and I want the system to generate an inspection point every 6 hours.

Is this possible? If so, how can it be done?

A. It is possible with 4.6C. You need a couple of function modules to do so and/or a report. See below:

In the QM customizing you can assign function modules per inspection point's definition.

1. Default for user fields in result recording:

Make use of FM QAPP_CUST_IP_PROPOSAL as a copy model and add functions to create inspection points according to your logic. For example, read the date and time of inspection lot creation and add 6 hours for the first/next inspection point. The FM will have the date/time accordingly as a default.

2. Automatic creation of insp. points:

From the SAP document:

You can use the available function module to generate inspection points for the inspection during production already when the inspection lot is created. This means you now have an alternative to creating inspection points manually during results recording.

3. Verification of user fields in results recording.
4. List of values for user fields in results recording.

Numbers 3 and 4 may not be relevant for your case.

Always read the documentation provided with the standard function modules to get an idea how they work. Also check the other available controls for inspection points.

To provide a full solution it is necessary to know more about your process. It will be important how your PP processes are defined. For example, how to identify the number of inspection points (start/end time of process order, quantity related maybe?).

It also might make sense to create a new inspection point on demand, e.g. when you valuate the latest inspection point, the system may create a new one (confirmation by pop-up). You may also want include a check if the related process order is not yet confirmed.

With more coding and some user-exits (need to check which one would be applicable) you can create a report, scheduled on a regular basis, creating inspection points in the background. This will be possible, but the personal for result recording need to know (applying refresh e.g. in QE51N).

Another hint: In case you automate the inspection point creation, deactivate the 'Default for next inspection point' (QE51N) so that the end user can not create manually inspected points. Define a standard variant and set the flag 'invisible'. Ensure that end users can not access standard variants.

SAP QM Interview Questions, Answers, and Explanations

Question 68: QM in Production

We want to implement QM in Production. Material during the production process is inspected every two hours.

What setting must we do if we want to record the inspection results?

A. What you described sounds like in-process-control.

In-Process-Control: Activate inspection type 03 in the QM view of the material master. Add inspection characteristics to your recipe. Make use of a proper inspection point ID. You might want to automate the creation of inspection points each 2 hours? Then you need some function modules for the inspection point ID (check the QM customizing).

End-process-control:
Activate inspection type 04 in the QM view. Create an inspection plan (check you're customizing for plan usage). Add inspection characteristics to the plan (assuming QM master data is already available) methods, characteristics, work center....). Release the plan. Check the additional features in the QM view for inspection type 04, like early inspection lot creation. From release 4.x you can assign inspection

points even to inspection type 04 and you can setup IPC with insp. type 04 as well.

It's all about your overall process. It's not always easy to provide a good solution.

Question 69: Digital Signatures and COA's

I'm trying to understand the process of creating a COA for an outbound delivery. The business requirement is for a digital signature to be created and printed on the COA. I'm not really sure of the whole digital signature process.

How can I comply with this?

A. For a bitmap signature you simply save the bitmap into a standard text object and have the SAP script form enter the appropriate signature based on some logic. This is usually the lab manager's signature for a plant.

If you are referring to an actual digital signature from interfaced hardware, you'll have to wait for someone else to respond.

There is no functionality known to me regarding a digital signature for an outbound COA.

You can incorporate digital signatures with UD. When I meant that digital signatures could be used, that was what I was referring to. The COA SAP script would have to look up the digital signature of the person that did the UD on the lot. Of course that can be a problem if you use Auto UD's.

The only way I suspect you could specifically show that the COA was reviewed and signed would be to somehow tie it to the Delivery document. Set the outputs to a timing of "3" - explicit request". The person reviewing the COA would do it via the delivery. When they are satisfied, they change the timing from a 3 to a 4 and save the delivery. You'd have to find a user exit here and some how tie your digital signature equipment in at this step. Capture the signature, and save it so that it now available for the COA SAP script forms.

SAP QM Interview Questions, Answers, and Explanations

Question 70: Changing Character Results after UD?

After entering characteristics results and giving UD, the user realizes that some of the entered results are wrong, despite the fact that they are in specification and the product had to be released for free usage.

How can I correct the result?

1) I couldn't reverse the UD;
2) No process on the inspection lot is allowed, except some new long term characteristic;

How do resolve this issue?

A. You cannot change inspection results once the UD has been made. While there are some OSS notes on how to get around this, SAP does not recommend it and does not support it.

Also go to the Change UD transaction for the original inspection lot and document in the UD text that a second lot was created to correct an incorrect result and reference the inspection lot number.

Create a new manual inspection lot, where the correct results will be stored.

Question 71: CPK value on a weekly/ daily basis

Our customers require a huge variety on CPK values for a couple of characteristics. Some want to get it per week, others per batch.

To my knowledge the 4.6c standard is only on a monthly base in MCXD.

I also see problems on creating a calculated characteristic, since when weekly base is required we talk about several process orders and several batches.

A similar thing applies to MCXB, which I would need on a daily and weekly basis.

Is it possible to customize something or does it need programming?

A. MCXD and MCXB are derived from the standard LIS structures and the period for analysis is a "Month". The only direct solution would be to go for a customer LIS by copying the standard with a different period to analyze. Be aware of the large amount of data records that these structures would be capturing, being on a daily basis.

For CPK, you may have to look at SPC charts and have the right SPC criterion or "close" the SPC charts periodically.

Question 72: Inspection Sample

We have a situation concerning the tracking of physical samples during the inspection process. Presently, we receive a lot of material either from vendor or production and they are placed in a physical quarantine location and are in quality stock in SAP pending test completion. Samples are pulled per sample drawing instructions and delivered to our labs located in another area of the plant. Samples pulled may be more or less than specified per the sample drawing instructions. It is possible that samples not consumed are returned to the lot contained in quarantine, scrapped or both. We have a requirement to demonstrate actual location of all inventories for a given material at any point in time. In the inspection lot change mode I navigated to inspection processing/sample management/maintain sample location.

Where can I find more information on this functionality or is there another alternative?

Preferably the sample would be seen on standard inventory reports as in quality stock but with different (lab) storage locations.

A. The Sample management component does not interact with inventory movements. The whole inspection lot will be considered at the storage location that was used for the GR. To be able to monitor stocks in a different location, you have to do inventory transfers (if you need to).

Always recollect that the sample location is only for the tracking and monitoring purpose and is linked with Inventory Management.

Question 73: Percentage inspection with points

We were using 100% inspection in our company earlier, so I used free inspection point indicator in routing header.

For one of the operations I want to use 20% sampling but I can not attach percent sampling procedure as it is not allowed with free inspection points.

Can we make some settings to use percentage sampling procedure with inspection pointss?

A. Yes you can. In the material master for 03 inspection type, deselect 100% inspection and enter in 20% in the field below, % inspection.

Question 74: No Inspection Lot after GR Production Order

I have one batch under QI status as a result of Good Receipt Production Order but no inspection lot created as it should be.

What should I do to move the batch from QI into unrestricted?

A. Is QM activated for the material? If not, use transaction MB1B, movement 321.

If QM is activated, you have an inspection lot. What has probably happened is that you've forgotten to maintain the task list or the material specifications. What you should do then is to maintain the task list/material spec. Go to "Change inspection lot", QA02, and use the search criteria (material & batch would normally do) to locate your inspection lot.

You'll probably find the status CRTD. Then go to the inspection specification tab strip and press the 'Select task list/specification' button.

The task list/specification is the N assigned to your lot, and you should get it on your work list.

Question 75: Certificate results from production chain

I want to create a COA containing results from the production chain measurements. Materials are only partly batch managed.

Were those measurement results which are assigned to a batch (link with a MIC and a class characteristic) able to be "counted in"? (I.e. only those results can be shown on the COA).

A. As long as the component (material in the production chain) is batch managed, you can pull in the results into the header certificate. In the certificate profile you define the origin of the data (whether the component batch supplies the result or the inspection lot that corresponds to the component batch).

You cannot fetch the component results if it is not batch managed. The production chain functionality works using the batch of used function modules.

Question 76: Activate inspection for SD

We are planning to activate inspection for SD. Which inspection should I assign to material? Is it 02 or 10? What are the differences between these inspection types? I'm using 4.6c.

If this inspection type were activated, when will inspection lot automatically be created, after SO creation or after DO?

A. If you want an inspection lot for specific sales order use 10, never 02. Do the IMG settings also. This is quite an extensive area so read the help files in net www.help.sap.com. For additional information, go to print files.

You must also create a Quality-info record in SD where you define whether UD should be carried out before delivery or can it be afterwards. Creating sales order doesn't activate anything. Even certificate is activated by picking the earliest time period.

Question 77: Inspection Plan Header / Change Parameters

We upgraded to 4.6.

We used to require a "change master" to update an Inspection Plan. However, I am encountering problems with Change rule & Change type under the label of Change Parameters (Inspection Plan header).

I am searching where to control this in IMG (presumed). I may be encountering a security problem.

How do I resolve this?

A. If you upgraded and your old plans used change control, then I think you're stuck with it. I think once change control documents exist for a plan, you can't remove change control for those plans. Thus, the system is requiring you to maintain the change control rules.

Question 78: Valuation for inspection point

I am in 4.OB.

I am using result recovery with inspection points, after recording inspected and non conforming units. When I try to save; something needs to be entered such as 'yield'. While doing so I have to manually change the confirmation indicator from partial or final confirmation to 'NO CONFIRMATION'.

As our company shop floor people enter confirmations, QM doesn't need to enter confirmation. But the data entry operator sometimes clicks on partial /final confirmation indicator. To avoid this i want to make no conf. as default. I.e. confirmation should be possible only from production order confirmation->operation->time ticket only.

How do I resolve this issue?

A. The control key does not control the confirmations from a QM/PP perspective.

Go into the details of the operation. Under the section Quality Management inspection point there is a field inspection point completion. This controls the

ns/process order.
integration between the inspection point and the production/process order.

Question 79: Contact in Quality notification for Q4

In order to create and print a form out of a Q4 notification in 4.6c I need to enter customer number in contact person. For some reason some of the customer numbers do work, while others don't. I have absolutely no clue why this happens.

Could there be any setting in the customer master related to this?

In this notification, we use the sold-to-party. I have checked in OQN9, and that Q4 SP and CP are set.

Afterwards I have checked the settings in VD03 customer master and have found the customers where it is not working and have no partner function SP - only SH since they are subsidiaries.

If I changed the setting in OQN9 to SH for the sold-to-party, will it have any other effects?

A. Try to check which partner functions are allocated to "Customer" and
"Contact Person" in OQN9:
-Customer: SP
-Contact person: CP

It seems your Contact Person field is mandatory but why are you maintaining Customers in that field, rather than using the Sold-to-party field for Customers and the Contact person field for what is intended?

Just be aware that once you change the partner function to SH, system won't recognize SP. I'm not aware of any other direct implication.

Question 80: Collective inspection lot for batch

I've got the following scenario:

- We purchase a quantity, containing several batches from a vendor.
- Samples are removed of each batch and flown to our QC-dept, who analyze the samples and say OK.
- The quantity is then packed in several containers, and some batches will be split in two containers.
- The containers are shipped to different locations, and since transport is included in the price, we thus need to have each container as a separate line in the PO due to a different price.
- After the containers are shipped, SD-dept gets a list from the vendor telling us which batches are in which container (PO-line).
- We then do a GR in our 'main plant' (even though most containers will never appear there but go directly to other plants), and thus has to split each line in separate batches, before we transfer it on a stock transport order to the different plants used for distribution where they will be received in stock at the time of arrival.

My challenge is:

QC states that they approve each batch once, and for the full batch qty, thus demanding that we get ONE inspection lot for the whole qty.

SAP QM Interview Questions, Answers, and Explanations

But if a batch is split on two different PO-lines we'll get two GR, and two inspection lots.

I thought that source inspection might be the solution, but then I get one inspection lot for the whole container.

We're using 4.6c

A. Try to change your settings in the field "Lot for MatDocItem" to "2" (an inspection lot per material and batch) in your relevant inspection type (01) in Material Master. This should take care of your problems.

Question 81: Initial Load of QI Stock

What is the best way to load QI stock for the initial inventory load? I see a 563 movement type, but I get a hard error when I try to use it. It only changes the status of the stock within the QM module.

Is there any way to load QI stock and create the corresponding inspection lot automatically?

Do I need a special inspection type?

A. Version 4.6c has in the QM plant settings a field for setting the inspection type to be used for the initial stock load and automatic creation of the inspection lots. You can use 561 movement type.

Activate inspection type 05, Inspection for other goods receipt for the material.

Then your stock count will initiate an inspection lot.

You might also want to deactivate the inspection type after your stock count.

SAP QM Interview Questions, Answers, and Explanations

Question 82: Generate a new inspection lot if source lot is rejected

We have a source inspection lot rejected. The vendor re-offered the material.

How do I generate the lot again for the same material for the same PO?

A. You cannot do an inspection lot again if a UD is carried out. The easiest way is to create a manual inspection lot and write a reference to the rejected source inspection lot.

You can also use a follow up action called in the UD by a usage decision code to recreate a new inspection lot with the same parameters than the inspection lot.

This follow up action will call a custom function to recreate an inspection lot using the standard module: QPL1_INSPECTION_LOT_CREATE.

The dvp of this function was quite complex but it works.

Question 83: User Exit for QA11

We are on version 3.1I and need to start a process depending on the outcome of the UD.

Is there a user exit in QA11?

A. The easiest way to do this is with a follow-up function. In the configuration, link a function module to a follow-up action name. Then in the selected set for the UD codes select the proper follow-up action for each code.

Question 84: Partial lots - Urgent

I am facing a problem. I would like to make a UD for the partial lots which have been produced in different shifts. The business scenario requires that UD for partial lots is to be made. I am able to make a UD for the whole lot but not for the partial lots.

Is there any IMG setting available or if not, how do I resolve this?

A. You can make a usage decision for individual partial lots or for several selected partial lots collectively. You cannot make a usage decision for a partial lot if:

The status of the partial lot does not allow the inspection to be completed, a usage decision to be made, or the usage decision to be changed, or if samples are currently being processed for the partial lot.

If you decide to make a usage decision for the entire inspection lot instead of a partial lot, the usage decision also applies. You cannot define follow-up actions for partial lots.

Check the status of the partial lots. If your scenario is to simply record inspections based on shifts, then why not just have a new inspection lot created for each GR instead. At the end of each shift the material is receipted and a 04 inspection lot is created.

Question 85: Formula in Function Module

I need to do a complex calculation in a MIC: lineal regression. I know that is possible to use the Function Module in SAP.

How I can use this module to add this kind of formula?

A. In configuration you have to assign the function module to a formula parameter like Z1. Then when you create the MIC set the control indicators for a calculated characteristic. When the characteristic is added to an inspection plan, the system should force you to a "formula" field. In this field you simply have to enter Z1 or Z1xxxx where xxxx is the characteristic in the plan to get the input values from.

Z1 tells the system to use the function module configured to do whatever you wrote the function module to do, using another characteristic value as the input and sending back as output some value for your calculated characteristic.

Question 86: Confirmation in result recording

I want to display "no-confirmation indicator" as default during result recording, for one of the material maintains in plant 1. But for other material maintained in plant 2 " partial conf " is appearing as default. I have checked customizing settings in production-> prod orders-> operations-> confirmation settings are the same for both plants.

How do I trace the possible cause of error?

A. You want to look at the recipe/order and into the QM settings. Somewhere in there is the setting for the confirmation. The control key for the operation can affect this as well.

Question 87: QM & ISO

Can we use QM module to control the process of developing and maintaining ISO documents and requirements?

This should include the following:
- Quality document control updates and versioning and distribution.
- Quality audit scheduling.
- Non-conformity reports.

A. There are ways to address these issues, but it depends on what release you are on. If you are using the newer products such as CRM - there is a fully developed Audit Management tool for the scheduling of audits (any kind of audit) in which you can create question lists and develop an Audit Plan. This Audit Management Tool is incorporated into the new Enterprise release. If you are using any of the older releases you can use the Inspection Planning process to develop your audit questions. One can also get clever by creating 'Dummy Materials' and 'Dummy Batches' and use Shelf Life Expiry to trigger your inspection lots (audits).

The standard Document Management System should take care of your ISO documents - including version control, etc.

Question 88: Test report analysis-changing

Is it possible to change test report analysis after user decision (UD) executed once.

A. Inspection results can't be changed after UD. SAP provides a user exit to cancel the UD but this is not recommended and easy to check that this is not active. So test reports can't be changed within standard coding.

Question 89: QM Notification screen exit

I have created a project using QQMA001 and add a field to my sub screen. Everything is working ok so far, but I am unable to put the field in display mode. When I go into transaction IW53 (to display) it is still in input mode.

I have tried using loop at screen etc. but it still does not work. The loop at screen code is in the user exit.

How do I fix this?

A. You should add the following code into the exit:

Import p_aktyp from memory id 'AKTYP';
Free memory id 'AKTYP';
If p_aktyp = 'A';
Loop at screen;
Move 0 to screen-input;
Modify screen;
End loop.

Question 90: One goods receipt inspection per vendor batch

After setting the Control inspection lot indicator in the QM view of the material master "For each material, batch and storage location", I observed the following:

At goods receipt when entering a previously entered batch number the system gives a warning rather than error that the batch has been previously stocked. Additional receipts for the batch add stock to the original inspection lot regardless of change over to another PO or line item as long as the material, batch and storage location remain constant. This occurs irregardless of original inspection lot status. The material/purchasing document assignment remains that of the first goods receipt.

Is there a way to perform only one goods receipt inspection per vendor batch as required to ensure quality?

A. The system is behaving as designed. The only problem is, it appears that way in your process, because the inspection was not completed before the second GR was done. The additional material was added to the existing inspection lot. This is as it should be. Why would you want the second material to go to unrestricted inventory "at risk"? After all, the batch hasn't been cleared yet.

Once you make a UD on the inspection lot, all additional receipts of the batch should go directly to unrestricted.

Question 91: Change of revision level with creation of inspection lot

We plan to use the revision level functionality to track changes on a specific part. We also want to inspect this part when the revision level changes. Let's say, the revision level of a part is A. The next lot is supposed to be a skip lot (according to my quality level) but meanwhile I changed the revision level of this part to B. I want SAP to create an inspection lot for the next lot that will be received even if this lot is supposed to be skipped.

Do you have an idea on how to force the system to create an inspection lot and pre-program when the revision will make changes?

A. I don't think there is an automatic way to do this in SAP. It would require some customization. Possibly through a user exit when you save the material.

Question 92: Document flow in QM notification

We have made quite long chain (7) in notifications and now these notifications which are in the beginning don't appear in document flow. There is also one PM notification in the beginning of the chain. So it seems that only 6 notifications can be seen.

Is it possible to account for the amount of notifications in sight?

A. The number of levels in document flow of QM notification is set when SAP call the function "SREL_GET_NEXT_RELATIONS", using the "Max_hops" parameter.

Problem: The value is set into the standard code.

Solution: You can install a note n° 177289 and 534308 in your system to set up the depth of document flow as you like.

Question 93: Inspection Activation at the time of Material Creation

We would like to have inspection setup populate with the creation of material dependent on material type.

Is there functionality available to assign and activate inspection types automatically at material creation based upon material types or any other parameters?

A. No. I'm afraid you can't do what you want.

You would need to a customized program to do that and probably custom tables to hold the default values you wish to use for each material type.

You could, instead create template materials. The template materials will contain the basic information you expect for a type of material. Then use these materials to copy from when you create a new material. All the values from the copied material would be used including the settings for the QM inspection types.

If you have an automatic program for creating materials, it could be reprogrammed to use the template materials as the starting point.

SAP QM Interview Questions, Answers, and Explanations

Question 93: Inspection Lot stuck between QM & WM

After making a usage decision against an inspection lot and posting the correct amount on the Inspection stock screen within QA11, this stock should be transferred to unrestricted within WM. Posting change in IM worked, but it didn't automatically process a posting change in WM. This is shown by a visible open item on LU04. For the movement type in configuration create automatic transfer is set to 2. This applies to a 321 movement.

How do I fix this problem?

A. If it is one lot alone, then check OSS. There are notes in there concerning problems between WM/IM and QM stock. SAP provides a program to correct this. For systems prior to 4.0 you have to apply the OSS note. In 4.0 the program is provided in the system and I believe in 4.6 it was actually given a transaction code.

Question 94: Quality score attached to material

My client has this particular requirement:

During material check, if the quality were under acceptance level, they never reject the material; only put the score on lower level.

The question is, can we map this requirement into SAP system?

Since the material number will be only one, but they will differentiate this material under several quality levels (e.g. material A will be divided into several classes based on quality score, say 100, 90, 80 and 70). If this is possible, what should I set on the system?

A. If you are using batch management, then you could potentially transfer the score through QM to the classification. Then use batch determination to select material batches appropriately, depending on their Quality Score.

Question 95: Block Stock to Unrestricted Stock

After taking UD as rejected, and moved to block stock, I wanted to accept the lot by changing UD and take it to unrestricted stock but was not allowed. I was allowed to change UD code only.

How do I move the stock after rejection to block stock?

I can do it by MB1B and move the stock to unrestricted but how can we move it from QA12?

A. You can't. Once the stock posting is done, it is done. The standard SAP way is to move the material using standard stock movements. If you want to automate it, consider a follow-up action. The follow-up action determines if this is a change of the UD and then it makes the appropriate stock move in the background for you.

Be warned. It could be very difficult to get this working right and you may find times you don't want the follow-up action to take place, so you may need several UD codes to give you various options.

Question 96: Action Box component - Create Quality Notification

I need some advice on doing some work with the action box items in Quality Notifications.

We have configured the Service Notifications to create a Quality Notification from the Action Box of the Service Notification. The Problem is that although this works perfectly in our sandbox environment, it will not work in the TEST environment, despite identical configuration and user authorizations. I'm wondering if there is something on a Basis or technical side that affects how the Function Module (QM06_FM_TASK_CREATE_QM_NOTIFIC) or the associated background Workflow Task (TS20000304) operate that could be different between a Sandbox and a TEST environment, or is there something else I need to learn about using FM's?

A. There was an issue with the Workflow customizing that prevented the automatic creation of the Notifications from the Action Box. Once the Workflow customizing was properly set, everything will work perfectly even to the point of executing all the previously unsuccessful attempts sitting in a buffer or a queue somewhere.

SAP QM Interview Questions, Answers, and Explanations

Run the SWU3 Workflow verification to check for errors.

This function module uses the workflow runtime system. In the IMG "Maintain Standard settings for SAP Business Workflow" (SWU3) the upper half has to be OK (RFC settings, WF-BATCH user & job etc.).

Question 97: Skipped inspection lots and quality certificate

I wonder if it would be possible to print a quality certificate for batches where inspection lot is skipped. For example, the material is produced with five different batches per day but only one batch is inspected (inspection lot is created for each batch). What happens if I want to print out quality certificate for the second batch?

How can I link the other batches to produce one result?

A. I think you have to create a function module for this with your rules for selecting the result. SAP provides one rule to get the results from the batch when the lot is a skip lot. If your batch has no values, (which is kind of a bad thing in most cases), then you can configure another choice for this and add the function module. Your function module should then include your rules for which results to report.

It is best to get a process in place where by ALL batches have a result i.e. a batch job, or follow up action after a UD that populates related batches. Then on the skip lots, we get the results from the batch.

SAP QM Interview Questions, Answers, and Explanations

Question 98: User defined screens in Notification 090 Customer sub screen

I would like to create tabs in the notification with user defined fields.

How does one create a Customer sub screen (customer exit QQM0100) in the notification?

Can one change the standard field descriptions on other screens?

How does one use this customer exit?

A. First of all, create enhancement.

For a normal enhancement these are the usual steps:

1. Create a project in CMOD and assign enhancement QQM0100;
2. Check in SMOD for function module/component in QQM0100;
3. Create your Z***** include for function module in SE37;
4. Go to CMOD again and activate project;

The second step is to change the field description.

To change standard descriptions in 40b: CMOD > Text Enhancements > Keywords > Change;

You might need to force the screen to be updated by re-generating the screen in SE51 pressing Ctrl+F3.

Question 99: Text for auto UD in batch record

When an automatic UD is performed a text saying that the UD was performed automatically is added to the batch record. I would like to stop this function for reporting reasons.

Can this be done easily or is it necessary to do it with some coding?

A. There is no easy way to stop this easily. I would assume however that it should be easy enough for a developer to use debug to locate the line that outputs that text and comment it out. Document it well as every upgrade or hot pack could potentially undo your work.

SAP QM Interview Questions, Answers, and Explanations

Transaction Codes

Q000   Quality management
QA00   Quality inspection
QA01   Create Inspection Lot
QA01A   Create Inspection Lot
QA02   Change Inspection Lot
QA02A   Change Inspection Lot
QA03   Display inspection lot
QA05   Job planning: Periodic inspection
QA06   Job overview: Periodic inspection
QA07   Trigger for recurring inspection
QA07L   Deadline Monitoring Log
QA08   Collective Processing of Insp. Setup
QA09   No. range maintenance for insp.lots
QA10   Trigger automatic usage decision
QA10L   Log for Automatic Usage Decision
QA11   Record usage decision
QA12   Change usage decision with history
QA13   Display usage decision
QA14   Change UD without history
QA16   Collective UD for accepted lots
QA17   Job planning for auto usage decision
QA18   Job overview for auto usage decision
QA19   Automatic usage decision
QA22   Change inspection point quantities
QA23   Display insp.point quantities
QA32   Change data for inspection lot
QA32WP QA32 -Call from Workplace/MiniApp
QA33   Display data for inspection lot
QA40   Auto. Usage Decision for Production
QA40L   Log for Automatic Usage Decision
QA41   Scheduling UD for Production Lots
QA42   Job planning: UD prod. insp.lots
QA51   Scheduling Source Inspections
QA52   Source inspections: Job overview
QAC1   Change insp. lot actual quantity
QAC2   Transfer stock to insp. lot
QAC3   Reset sample

149

SAP QM Interview Questions, Answers, and Explanations

QAER	Display archive objects
QAS1	Download Insp. Specs. (Obsolete)
QAS2	Download Basic Data (Obsolete)
QAS3	Upload Results (Obsolete)
QAS4	Upload UD (Obsolete)
QC01	Create certificate profile
QC02	Change certificate profile
QC03	Display certificate profile
QC06	Immediate delete of cert. profiles
QC11	Create cert. profile assignment
QC12	Change cert. profile assignment
QC13	Display cert. profile assignment
QC14	Create cert.prof.assign.w/copy model
QC15	Create cert. profile assignment
QC16	Change cert. profile assignment
QC17	Display cert. profile assignment
QC18	Create cert.prof.assign.w/copy model
QC20	Certificates for Deliveries
QC21	Quality certificate for the insp.lot
QC22	Quality Certificate for Batch
QC31	Archive display: Delivery item
QC32	Archive display: Inspection lot
QC40	Internet Certificate for Delivery
QC40A	Internet Certificate for Delivery
QC42	Batch certificate on WWW
QC51	Create certificate in procurement
QC52	Change certificate in procurement
QC53	Display certificate in procurement
QC55	Worklist: Certificates - Procurement
QCC0	QM: Direct Access to IMG
QCC1	Direct Access to IMG: Notification
QCC2	IMG Direct Access: QM Q-Notification
QCC3	IMG Direct Access: QM Q-Inspection
QCC4	IMG Direct Access: QM Q-Planning
QCC5	IMG Direct Selection: QM Bus. Add-In
QCC_STABI	Copy Stability Study Customizing
QCC_STABI_NK	Copy Stability Study Number Ranges
QCCC	QM standard settings complete
QCCF	QM standard forms
QCCK	QM standard settings: Catalogs
QCCM	QM std. settings: Qual. notifs.
QCCN	QM standard number ranges

QCCP	QM std. settings: Quality planning
QCCS	QM sampling schemes
QCCT	QM standard texts
QCCU	QM standard settings: Environment
QCCW	QM std. settings: Quality inspection
QCCY	Transport QM tolerance key
QCCZ	QM std. settings: Qual. certificates
QCE2	Edit Communication Support
QCE3	Display Communication Support
QCYF	QM standard forms (general)
QCYT	QM standard texts (general)
QD21	Mark completed notifications
QD22	Archiving Notifications: Archive
QD24	Archiving Notifications: Delete
QD25	Archiving Notifications: Admin.
QD33	Delete quality level
QD34	Delete quality level planning
QD35	Delete job overview for Q-levels
QDA1	Edit sampling type
QDA3	Display sampling type
QDB1	Maintain allowed relationships
QDB3	Display allowed relationships
QDH1	Q-level evaluation: Change data
QDH2	Q-level evaluation: Display data
QDL1	Create quality level
QDL2	Change quality level
QDL3	Display quality level
QDM1	Edit valuation mode
QDM3	Display valuation mode
QDP1	Create sampling scheme
QDP2	Change sampling scheme
QDP3	Display sampling scheme
QDR1	Create dynamic modification rule
QDR2	Change dynamic modification rule
QDR3	Display dynamic modification rule
QDR6	Disp. where-used list-dyn. mod. rule
QDR7	Replace dynamic mod. rule used
QDV1	Create sampling procedure
QDV2	Change sampling procedure
QDV3	Display sampling procedure
QDV6	Uses: Sampling procedures
QDV7	Replace sampling procedure used

151

SAP QM Interview Questions, Answers, and Explanations

QE00   Quality Planning
QE01   Record characteristic results
QE02   Change characteristic results
QE03   Display characteristic results
QE04   Record sample results
QE05   Change sample results
QE06   Display sample results
QE09   Indiv.display of charac.result
QE09WP Call QE09 from Workplace
QE11   Record results for inspection point
QE12   Change results for inspection point
QE13   Display results for inspection point
QE14   Record results for delivery note
QE15   Change results for delivery note
QE16   Display results for delivery note
QE17   Record results for equipment
QE18   Change results for equipment
QE19   Display results for equipment
QE20   Record results for funct. location
QE21   Change results for funct. location
QE22   Display results for funct. location
QE23   Record results for phys. sample
QE24   Change results for phys. sample
QE25   Display results for phys. sample
QE29   No. Range Maint.: Conf. No. for Char
QE51   Results recording worklist
QE51N   Results Recording Worklist
QE52   Worklist: Results for phys. sample
QE53   Worklist: Record results for equip.
QE54   Worklist: Results for funct. loctns
QE71   Tabular res. recording for insp. pts
QE72   Tabular Results Rec. for Insp. Lots
QE73   Tabular res. recording for characs.
QEH1   Worklist for Mobile Results Rec.
QEI1   Displaying QM Interfaces Appl. Log
QEI2   Deleting QM Interfaces Appl. Log
QEW01   Results Recording on Web
QEW01V Variant Maint.: Recording on Web
QF01   Record defect data
QF02   Change defect data
QF03   Display defect data
QF11   Record defects for inspection lot

SAP QM Interview Questions, Answers, and Explanations

QF21 Record defects for operation
QF31 Record defects for characteristic
QG09 Maint. num. range Q control charts
QGA1 Display quality score time line
QGA2 Display inspection results
QGA3 Print inspection results
QGC1 Qual. control charts for insp. lots
QGC2 Control charts for task list charac.
QGC3 Control charts for master insp. char
QGD1 Test Equipment Usage List
QGD2 Test Equipment Tracking
QGP1 Results history for task list charac
QGP2 Results History for Task List Charac
QI01 Create quality info. - purchasing
QI02 Change qual.information - purchasing
QI03 Display quality info. - purchasing
QI04 Job planning for QM procurement keys
QI05 Mass maintenance QM procurement keys
QI06 QM Releases: Mass maintenance
QI07 Incoming insp. and open pur. orders
QI08 Job overview of QM procurement keys
QISR Internal Service Request
QISR1 Internal Service Request - Forms
QISR_PCR60 vc_scenario for Message type 60(PCR)
QISR_SM29 ISR Customizing: Table Transfer
QISR_SR12_START Suggestion System
QISRSCENARIO Customizing Szenario
QISRTRANSPORT ISR Customizing Transport
QISRW Internal Service Request on the Web
QK01 Assign QM order to material
QK02 Display assigned QM orders
QK03 Maintain specs. for order type
QK04 Create QM order
QK05 Confirmed activities for insp. lot
QL11 Mat: Distribute Inspection Setup-ALE
QL21 Master Inspection Characs (ALE)
QL31 Distribute Inspection Methods (ALE)
QL41 Distribute Code Groups (ALE)
QM00 Quality Notifications
QM01 Create quality notification
QM02 Change quality notification
QM03 Display quality notification

153

QM10   Change list of quality notifications
QM10WP QM10 - Call from Workplace/MiniApp
QM11   Display List of Qual. Notifications
QM12   Change list of tasks
QM13   Display list of tasks
QM13WP QM13 - Call from Workplace/MiniApp
QM14   Change list of items
QM15   Display list of items
QM16   Change activity list
QM17   Display activity list
QM19   List of Q Notifications, Multi-Level
QM50   Time line display Q notifications
QMW1   Create quality notification (WWW)
QP01   Create
QP02   Change
QP03   Display
QP05   Print inspection plan
QP06   List: Missing/unusable insp. plans
QP07   List: Missing/Unusable GR InspPlans
QP08   Print task lists for material
QP11   Create reference operation set
QP12   Change reference operation set
QP13   Display reference operation set
QP48   Number Ranges for Physical Samples
QP49   Number range for phys. samp. drawing
QP60   Time-related development of plans
QP61   Display change documents insp.plan
QP62   Change documents ref.operation sets
QPIQS8 QM MiniApp Selection Variant
QPIQS9 QM MiniApp Selection Variant
QPNQ   Number ranges for inspection plans
QPQA32 QM MiniApp Selection Variant
QPQGC1 QM MiniApp Selection Variant
QPQM10 QM MiniApp Selection Variant
QPQM13 QM MiniApp Selection Variant
QPR1   Create physical sample
QPR2   Change physical sample
QPR3   Display physical sample
QPR4   Confirm physical sample drawing
QPR5   Manual inspection lots for physSamps
QPR6   Create new phys.-samp. drawing w.ref
QPR7   Storage Data Maintenance

QPV2	Maintain sample drawing procedure
QPV3	Display sample drawing procedure
QS21	Create master insp. characteristic
QS22	Create master insp. charac. version
QS23	Change master insp. charac. version
QS24	Display master insp. charac. version
QS25	Delete master insp. charac. version
QS26	Display characteristic use
QS27	Replace master insp. characteristic
QS28	Display insp. charac. list
QS29	Maintain characteristic number range
QS31	Create inspection method
QS32	Create inspection method version
QS33	Change inspection method version
QS34	Display inspection method version
QS35	Delete inspection method version
QS36	Display inspection method use
QS37	Central replacement of methods
QS38	Display inspection method list
QS39	Maintain method number range
QS41	Maintain catalog
QS42	Display catalog
QS43	Maintain catalog
QS44	Maintain catalog
QS45	Display catalog
QS46	Display code group use
QS47	Central replacement of code groups
QS48	Usage indicator - code groups
QS49	Display code groups and codes
QS4A	Display catalog
QS51	Edit Selected Sets
QS52	Display selected set index
QS53	Maintain individual selected set
QS54	Maintain selected set
QS55	Display selected set
QS58	Usage indicator - selected sets
QS59	Display selected sets
QS61	Maintain material specification
QS62	Display material specification
QS63	Maintain material spec: Planning
QS64	Display material spec: For key date
QS65	Activate material specification

QS66	Plan activation of material spec.
QS67	Job overview: Activate mat. spec.
QSR5	Archive inspection plans
QSR6	Delete routings
QST01	Create Stability Study
QST03	Display Stability History
QST04	Display Inspection Plans
QST05	Graphical Scheduling Overview
QST06	Scheduling Overview (StabilityStudy)
QST07	Change Testing Schedule Items
QST08	Display Testing Schedule Items
QSUB	Define subsystems
QT00	Test Equipment Management
QT01	Test equipment management
QTSA	Product Allocations: Send Quantities
QTSP	Product Allocations:Send Customizing
QUERY_BP_FSBPBILDER	BP: Screen Customizing for Query
QV01	Create quality assurance agreement
QV02	Change quality assurance agreement
QV03	Display quality assurance agreement
QV04	Find Quality Assurance Agreement
QV11	Create technical delivery terms
QV12	Change technical delivery terms
QV13	Display technical delivery terms
QV14	Search technical terms of delivery
QV21	Create QA agreement (DocType Q03)
QV22	Change Q-agreement (doc. type Q03)
QV23	Display Q-agreement (doc. type Q03)
QV24	Find Q-agreement (doc. type Q03)
QV31	Create Q-spec. (doc.type Q04)
QV32	Change Q-specification (docType Q04)
QV33	Displ. Q-specification (docType Q04)
QV34	Find Q-specification (doc. type Q04)
QV51	Create control for QM in SD
QV52	Change control for QM in SD
QV53	Display control for QM in SD
QVM1	Inspection lots without completion
QVM2	Inspection lots with open quantities
QVM3	Lots without usage decision
QZ00	Quality Certificates

SAP QM Interview Questions, Answers, and Explanations

Important Tables

Area Table Description
Master Data QMAT Inspection type - material parameters
Master Data QMHU QM Link Between Inspection Lot and Handling Unit Item
Master Data QMTB Inspection method master record
Master Data QMTT Inspection Method Texts
Master Data QPAC Inspection catalog codes for selected sets
Master Data QPAM Inspection catalog selected sets
Master Data QPMK Inspection characteristic master
Master Data QPMT Master Inspection Characteristics Texts
Master Data QPMZ Assignment table - insp. methods/master insp. characteristic
Master Data TQ01D Authorization groups for QM master data
Master Data TQ01E Text authorization groups for QM master data
Master Data TQ21 Assignment of screens to screen groups
Master Data TQ25 QM:screen sequence for master and inspection characteristics
QM Master Data

Catalog QPCD Inspection catalog codes
Catalog QPCT Code texts
Catalog QPGR Inspection catalog code groups
Catalog QPGT Code group texts

SAP QM Interview Questions, Answers, and Explanations

Catalog TQ07 Follow-Up Action for Usage Decision of Inspection Lot
Catalog TQ07A QM: Function Modules for Follow-Up Action
Catalog TQ07T Language-dependent texts for Table TQ07
Catalog TQ15 Inspection catalog type index
Catalog TQ15T Language-dependent texts for table TQ15
Catalog TQ17 Defect classes
Catalog TQ17T Language-dependent texts for table TQ17
Catalog

Sample Determination QDEB Allwd. Relationships: Sampling Procedures/Dynamic Mod. Rules
Sample Determination QDEBT Allowed combinations of procedures/dynamic mod. rules: texts
Sample Determination QDPA Sampling scheme-instructions
Sample Determination QDPK Sampling scheme header
Sample Determination QDPKT Sampling scheme: texts
Sample Determination QDPP Sampling scheme item
Sample Determination QDQL Quality level
Sample Determination

Inspection Char TQ17A Weighting of Char
Inspection Char TQ11 Inspection Qualification
Inspection Char TQ29 Tolerance Keys
Inspection Char T006 Unit of measurement
Inspection Char

Dynamic Modification QDBM Valuation mode
Dynamic Modification QDBMT Valuation Mode: Texts
Dynamic Modification QDDR Dynamic modification rule (header)
Dynamic Modification QDDRT Dynamic modification rule: texts
Dynamic Modification QDEP Allowed inspection severities
Dynamic Modification QDEPT Allowed Inspection Severities: Texts
Dynamic Modification QDFB Function modules for the individual procedure categories
Dynamic Modification QDFBT Function Modules for Procedure: Texts
Dynamic Modification QDFM Function modules for valuation mode
Dynamic Modification QDFMT Function Modules for Valuation Mode: Texts
Dynamic Modification QDPS Inspection stages for a dynamic modification rule
Dynamic Modification QDPST Inspection Stages: Texts
Dynamic Modification QDSA Sampling type
Dynamic Modification QDSAT Sampling Type: Texts
Dynamic Modification QDSV Sampling procedure
Dynamic Modification QDSVT Sampling Procedure: Texts
Dynamic Modification TQ39B QM : Activates reference for dyn. modification level
Dynamic Modification

Graphics & SPC QASH Quality control chart
Graphics & SPC QAST Control chart track
Graphics & SPC QPSH Control chart types

159

Graphics & SPC QPSHT Texts for control chart types
Graphics & SPC QPSP SPC criterion
Graphics & SPC QPSPT Texts for SPC criteria
Graphics & SPC QPST Control chart track
Graphics & SPC QPSTT Texts for control chart tracks
Graphics & SPC

Specifications QMSP QM: material specification
Specifications

Inspection Plan PLKO Inspection plan Header
Inspection Plan MAPL Material Assignement
Inspection Plan PLPO Operation Details
Inspection Plan PLMK Inspection plan characteristics
Inspection Plan PLMW MAPL-Dependent Charac. Specifications (Inspection Plan)
Inspection Plan TQ03 QSS: Control for Screen Texts/TABLE NOT USED (Rel. 4.6)
Inspection Plan TQ29A Dependency tolerance key-nominal measurement
Inspection Plan TQ72 Type of share calculation
Inspection Plan TQ72T Texts for type of share calculation
Inspection Plan TQ75 QM formula parameters
Inspection Plan TQ75F Field names for QM formulas
Inspection Plan TQ75K Short text for Table TQ75F
Inspection Plan TQ75T Description of formula parameters
Inspection Plan

Qm in procurement QINF QM-info record for material and vendor
Qm in procurement TQ02 QM system definition
Qm in procurement TQ02A QM system assignment and QM system requirements

SAP QM Interview Questions, Answers, and Explanations

Qm in procurement TQ02B QM system
Qm in procurement TQ02T QM system description
Qm in procurement TQ02U Description QM system
Qm in procurement TQ04A Functions that can be blocked
Qm in procurement TQ04S QM block functions : texts
Qm in procurement TQ05 QM certificate categories for procurement
Qm in procurement TQ05T QM: text table for certificate types
Qm in procurement TQ08 Control of QM in procurement
Qm in procurement TQ08T QM: text for QM procurement keys
Qm in procurement TQ09 QM: agreement of QM document types
Qm in procurement TQ09T QM: agreement of QM document types
Qm in procurement TQ32A Inspection type to status assignment from status profile
Qm in procurement

QM in SD QVDM QM Info Record - QM Control in SD
QM in SD TQ32B Find insp.type for quality insp. for delivery note
QM in SD

Inspectio lot QALS Inspection lot record
Inspectio lot QALT Partial lot
Inspectio lot T156Q Movement Type: Material-Independent Control
Inspectio lot TQ30 Inspection types
Inspectio lot TQ30T Texts for inspection types

SAP QM Interview Questions, Answers, and Explanations

Inspectio lot TQ32 Assignment of inspection type to origin
Inspectio lot TQ32C Lot creation allowed values for the origin
Inspectio lot TQ32C _T Texts for lot creation indicator
Inspectio lot TQ33 Relevant fields for origin
Inspectio lot TQ34 Default values for inspection type
Inspectio lot

Inspection point QAPP Inspection point
Inspection point TQ79 Table with inspection point/user field combinations
Inspection point TQ79T Key words for inspeciton point user fields
Inspection point

Results Recording QAES Sample unit table
Results Recording QAKL Results table for value classes
Results Recording QAMR Characteristic results during inspection processing
Results Recording QAMV Characteristic specifications for inspection processing
Results Recording QASE Results table for the sample unit
Results Recording QASR Sample results for inspection characteristics
Results Recording QASV Sample specifications for inspection processing
Results Recording TQ12 Ind. external numbering for test units in results recording
Results Recording TQ12T Texts for the ind. for ext. numbering of units to be insp.
Results Recording TQ70 Control table for results

recording
Results Recording TQ70C Function codes for navigation from the char.overview screen
Results Recording TQ70E Screen-based processing tables
Results Recording TQ70F Navigation during results recording
Results Recording TQ70S Characteristic overview screen for results recording
Results Recording TQ73 Origin of results data
Results Recording TQ73T Texts for origin of results data
Results Recording TQ74 Recording configuration
Results Recording TQ74T Recording configuration
Results Recording TQ76 Processing status of inspection characteristics
Results Recording TQ76T Texts for the processing status of insp. characteristics
Results Recording TQ77 Attributes for the Inspection Characteristic
Results Recording TQ77T Text Tables for Attributes
Results Recording TQ78 Status-dependent processing table for insp. characteristics
Results Recording TQ78T Texts for the status-specific proc. table for insp. char.
Results Recording

Defects recording TQ84 Confirmation profile
Defects recording TQ84T Text table for confirmation profile
Defects recording TQ86 Report category for defects recording
Defects recording TQ86A Assignment report category for work center
Defects recording TQ86T Text table for report

category
Defects recording V_T35 2B_F Generated table for view V_T352B_F
Defects recording

Usage decision QAMB QM: Link Between Inspection Lot and Material Document
Usage decision QAVE Inspection processing: Usage decision
Usage decision TQ06 Procedure for Calculating the Quality Score
Usage decision TQ06T Language-specific texts for Table TQ06
Usage decision TQ07M QM: Inventory postings with usage decision
Usage decision

Sample Mgmt QPRN Sample drawing of phys. samples
Sample Mgmt QPRS Master record for phys. samples
Sample Mgmt QPRVK Sample-drawing procedure
Sample Mgmt QPRVK T Header for sample drawing procedure texts
Sample Mgmt QPRVP Sample-drawing items
Sample Mgmt QPRVP T Items for sample drawing procedure texts
Sample Mgmt TQ40 Definition of sample types
Sample Mgmt TQ40T Text table for sample type
Sample Mgmt TQ41 Storage locations for physical samples
Sample Mgmt TQ41T Texts for storage locations
Sample Mgmt TQ42 Physical sample containers
Sample Mgmt TQ42T Texts for phys. sample containers
Sample Mgmt

QMIS S068 Vendor statistics
QMIS S069 Material statistics
QMIS S097 QM notifications: Matl anal.
QMIS S098 QM notification: Vendor anal.
QMIS S099 QM notifications: Cust. anal.
QMIS S100 Problems: Material analysis
QMIS S102 Problems: Vendor analysis
QMIS S103 Problems: Customer analysis
QMIS S104 Customer statistics
QMIS S161 Inspection results: General
QMIS S162 Quantitative insp. results
QMIS S163 Quant. Insp. Result: Vendor
QMIS S164 Quant. Insp. Result: Vendor
QMIS S165 Inspection result: gen. custs
QMIS S166 Insp. Results: Quant. Customer
QMIS TQ55 Assign inspection lot origin for update group
QMIS TQ56 Definition of quality score classes
QMIS TQ56T Text table for the definition of quality score classes
QMIS TQ57 Assignment of quality score key to info structure
QMIS

Quality Certificates QCPR QM quality certificates in procurement
Quality Certificates I000 Conditions for certificate profile
Quality Certificates KONDI Conditions: Data part for certificates
Quality Certificates QCVK Certificate profile header
Quality Certificates QCVM Certificate profile characteristic level
Quality Certificates QCVMT Certificate profile characteristic level: texts

Quality Certificates QCVV Certificate Profile: List of Preliminary Products
Quality Certificates TQ61 Result value origin for certificates
Quality Certificates TQ61T Origin of result values for certificates: texts
Quality Certificates TQ62 Output strategy for skip characteristics
Quality Certificates TQ62T Output strategy for skip characteristics: texts
Quality Certificates TQ63 Origin of insp. specs for certificates (function modules)
Quality Certificates TQ63T Origin of inspection specifications for certificates: texts
Quality Certificates TQ64 Origin of characteristic short text for certificates
Quality Certificates TQ64T Origin of characteristic short text for certificates: texts
Quality Certificates TQ65 Certificates: Combinations allowed for origins, specs/values
Quality Certificates TQ67 Certificate-Relevant Output Types
Quality Certificates

Quality Notification QMEL Notification header
Quality Notification QMFE Item
Quality Notification QMSM Task
Quality Notification QMMA Activities
Quality Notification T352C Catalog types for each catalog profile
Quality Notification TQ81 Notification Scenario
Quality Notification TQ81V Usage of parts
Quality Notification TQ81V_T Texts for usage of parts
Quality Notification TQ81_T Texts for Notification

166

Scenarios
Quality Notification TQ82 Change of Notification Type
Quality Notification TQ83 Partner Functions for Codes
Quality Notification TQ85 Function table for follow-up functions
Quality Notification TQ85R Rules for Follow-Up Functions
Quality Notification TQ85_T Action box text table
Quality Notification TQ8CO Assignment of reference orders to notification type
Quality Notification

Other Objects MARA Material Number
Other Objects T001W Plant
Other Objects LFA1 Vendor
Other Objects KNA1 Customer
Other Objects AUFK Order Number
Other Objects SAFK Run Schedule Header Number
Other Objects MCH1 Batch Number
Other Objects MCHA Batch Record
Other Objects EKKO Purchasing Document Header
Other Objects EKPO Purchasing document Item
Other Objects EKET Delivery Schedule
Other Objects VBUK Delivery Header
Other Objects VBUP Delivery Item
Other Objects CSKS Cost Center
Other Objects EQUI Equipment Number

Question 100: QM-QN-NT: creation of quality notice with reference to invoice

Our commercial systems want to register customer complaints in our SAP system. We decided to use QM. We are in 4.6C version. We can create a quality notice to a partner, to a delivery, and to an order.

Is it possible to create a quality notice to a customer invoice?

A. If this is your invoice to the customer it should link to the sales order.

In any case, you could use the Reference Number field VIQMEL-REFNUM - it's a free entry field but can be used easily in searches, so it's quite powerful.

SAP QM Interview Questions, Answers, and Explanations

SAP QM Interview Questions, Answers, and Explanations

Activate inspection 118
auto UD 149
Automate Inspection Points 104
Automatic closing 87
Automatic lot creation 65
batch generation 85
batch managed 117
Batch status 75
Batches 64
block stock 100
Block Stock 143
C202 29
Cancellation of inspection lots 82
Certificate results 117
Character Results 111
characteristics 77
Close Production Order 92
COA 117
Collective inspection 124
Collective Usage Decision 32
configuration 131
Confirmation profiles 101
Contact 6, 122, 123
Customer - material 50
Deactivate QM inspection 83
Digital Signatures 109
Document flow 139
ECN 53
engineering change functionality 52
External processing inspection 81
Extra posting proposal 36
follow-up function 128
formula 131, 161

170

Function Module 131
goods receipt 6, 11, 12, 22, 30, 99, 126, 136
GR Blocked stock.. 14
GR Production Order... 116
info record 22
In-process Inspection 29
in-process-control 107
Inspection Activation 140
inspection interval.. 40, 44
inspection lot
    change status 60
Inspection lot 31
Inspection Lot 17
inspection lot quantity.. 99
Inspection Lot stuck... 141
inspection lots.. 84
    automatic creation... 58
Inspection of material... 42
Inspection Origin 15
Inspection Plan Header................................ 6, 119
inspection plans 52
inspection point 4, 6, 33, 47, 104, 105, 106, 107, 115, 120, 150, 153, 163
Inspection Sample 113
Inspection Stock 4, 46
inspection type... 70
Invoice quantity... 21
ISO... 133
Long Term Inspection 98
Long text history.. 28
lot quantity 18
material master.... 22, 40, 44, 56, 59, 64, 77, 84, 107, 115, 136
Material Spec-Usage 77

Entry	Page
MB1B	116
MCXD	112
MM-IM	10
MM-PUR	10
Movement types	3, 15, 65
OQN9	122
Partial lots	6, 129
Payment control	37
pending Inspection Lot Number	54
Percentage inspection	115
Poor Quality Production	94
process order	46
Production	107
production chain	117
production confirmation	47
Production order	39
purchase order	22, 70, 83
QA11	6, 14, 21, 54, 80, 128, 141, 150
QC20	34
QE51N	106
QI stock	14
QI Stock	6, 126
QM Certificates	3, 39
QM in Delivery	89
QM notification	7, 139, 165
QM Notification	135
QM tables	62
QM01	43
QS34	90
quality documents	11
quality notification	49
Quality Notification	144
Quality score	142
QVM3	24, 54

SAP QM Interview Questions, Answers, and Explanations

Recording Defects 103
rejected 127
Release status 63
result recording 132
revision level 138
routes 5, 96
Sample management component 113
sample size 56
SE51 148
security 43
Serial numbers 99
Shelf life 40
Skip lots 59
Skipped inspection lots 146
stock movements 16
Stock posting tab 29
Stock postings 24
supply relationships 10, 11
Test report 134
Transaction Codes 150
upper limit 48
Usage decision 69
Usage Decision document 14
User defined screens 147
User Exit 4, 6, 49, 128
Valuation 5, 6, 78, 120, 159
vendor 4, 6, 11, 21, 42, 49, 61, 67, 68, 71, 72, 113, 124, 127, 136, 161
Vendor blocked 67
Vendor Evaluation 10, 49
Vendor Release 10
workflow 73

Printed in the United States
66871LVS00003B/86